The UK Instant Pot Vortex

Air Fryer Cookbook

Plenty of Easy, Quick and Delicious Recipes to Fry, Grill, and Roast with Your Instant Pot Vortex Air Fryer

Kari Forbes

Notice Of Disclaimer.

Please note that the information in this document is intended for educational and entertainment purposes only. Every effort has been made to provide accurate, up-to-date, reliable and complete information. No warranty of any kind is declared or implied. The reader acknowledges that the author does not engage in the provision of legal, financial, medical or professional advice. The content in this book has been obtained from a variety of sources. Please consult a licensed professional before attempting any of the techniques described in this book. By reading this document, the reader agrees that in no event shall the author be liable for any direct or indirect damages, including but not limited to errors, omissions or inaccuracies, resulting from the use of the information in this document.

CONTENTS

Fundamentals of the Instant Vortex Air Fryer Oven 10

What Is Instant Vortex Air Fryer Oven? 10

Main Functions of Instant Vortex Air Fryer Oven 10

The Benefits of Using Instant Vortex Air Fryer Oven 12

Breakfast Recipes 13

Biscuits With Smoked Sausage 13

Sweet Corn Muffins 13

Vegetable And Sausage Frittata 13

Mom's Cheesy Biscuits 14

Cheesy Egg Cups 14

Loaded Hash Browns 14

Classic Banana Beignets 15

Peppery Breakfast Quiche 15

Vanilla Pear Beignets 15

Scotch Eggs With Sausage 16

Favorite Pizza Sandwich 16

Grandma's Apple Fritters 16

Baked Pita Bread 17

Traditional Polish Naleśniki 17

Traditional Greek Tiganites 17

Mustard Cheese Sandwich 18

Mediterranean-style Cornbread Muffins 18

Fall Pumpkin Pancakes 18

Classic Breakfast Frittata 19

Greek-style Pita Pizza 19

Appetizers And Snacks Recipes 20

The Best Cheese Broccomole 20

Smoky Carrot Dip 20

Honey Apple Chips 20

Savory Herb Walnuts 21

Cheesy Broccoli Tots 21

Classic Parsnip Fries 21

Peppery Bean Dip 22

Restaurant-style Onion Rings 22

Montreal Chicken Drumettes 22

Cheese Broccoli Dip 23

Cheese Prawn Wontons 23

Italian Cheese Sticks 23

Sausage Wonton Wraps 24

Favorite Cauliflower Tots 24

Red Beetroot Chips 24

Kid-friendly Cheese Bites 25

Garlicky Broccoli Florets 25

Traditional Japanese Korokke 25

Brussel Sprout Chips 26

Texas-style Fried Pickles 26

Pork And Beef Recipes 27

Authentic Kansas City Strip 27

Roasted Boston Butt 27

Italian-style Pulled Pork 27

Orange Chuck Roast With Baby Potatoes 28

Breaded Filet Mignon 28

Jamaican-style Pork 28

Classic Homemade Cheeseburgers 29

Traditional Greek Keftedes 29

Pork And Sausage Patties 29

Classic Porterhouse Steaks 30

Crispy Pork Tenderloin 30

Entrecôte Steak With Cauliflower 30

Sriracha Pork Burgers 31

Beef Brisket With Brussels Sprouts 31

Blue Cheese-crusted Filet Mignon 31

Classic Beef Patties 32

Parmesan Pork Blade Chops 32

Festive Round Roast 33

Asian-style Beef Bowl 33

Festive Pork Butt 33

Fish And Seafood Recipes 34

Easy Catfish Sandwiches 34

Crab And Pea Patties 34

Favorite Halibut Steaks 34

Restaurant-style Fish Fingers 35

Greek-style Fish Sticks 35

Halibut Taco Wraps 35

Old Bay Pollock Fillets 36

Classic Fried Sea Scallops 36

Thai-style Shrimp 36

Lemony Sea Bass Fillets 37

Vegetable And Scallop Skewers 37

Mini Smoked Salmon Frittatas 37

Herbed Salmon Steaks 38

Hot Sardine Cutlets 38

Creole Catfish Fillets 38

Paprika Shrimp Salad 39

Street-style Fish Fritters 39

Father's Day Fish Tacos 39

Ultimate Tuna Melts 40

Favorite Seafood Fritters 40

Rice, Grains And Pastry Recipes 41

Greek-style Quinoa Croquettes 41

Chinese-style Rice Balls 41

Italian-style Oatmeal Cheeseburgers 41

Quiche Pastry Cups 42

Spelt Burgers With Herbs 42

Japanese-style Yaki Onigiri 42

Wild Rice Patties 43

Homemade Pita Chips 43

Buffalo-style Pizza 43

Spicy Oatmeal Patties 43

Corn Bacon Waffles 44

Mushroom And Oatmeal Fritters 44

Easy Pepperoni Pizza 45

Italian-style Mini Pies 45

Toasted Greek Pita 45

Classic Tortilla Chips 45

Easy Cinnamon Donuts 46

Easy Breakfast Granola 46

Mediterranean-style Calzone 46

Mexican-style Bulgur Patties 47

Poultry Recipes 47

Kid-friendly Chicken Nuggets 47

Juicy Turkey Breasts 48

Grandma's Chicken Roulade 48

Louisiana-style Stuffed Chicken 48

Classic Turkey Burgers 49

Paprika Roast Turkey 49

Kid-friendly Chicken Croquettes 49

Blue Cheese Chicken Drumettes 50

Herbed Chicken Drumsticks 50

Hot Chicken Drumettes 50

Classic Chicken Drumsticks 51

Classic Chicken Tacos 51

Bbq Chicken Legs 51

Creamed Chicken Salad 52

Turkey And Mushroom Croquettes 52

Chicken Fajita Salad 52

Authentic Chicken Fajitas 53

Mediterranean Chicken Salad 53

Chicken Sausage With Peppers 54

Traditional Moroccan Brochettes 54

Vegetables And Side Dishes Recipes 55

Italian-style Mushroom Patties 55

Roasted Pepper And Cheese Bowl 55

Grandma's Roasted Squash 55

Cheese-stuffed Mushrooms 56

Spicy Green Beans With Mushrooms 56

Golden Dijon Potatoes 56

Cheesy Roasted Parsnips 57

Fried Breaded Portobellas 57

Roasted Buttery Eggplant 57

Rainbow Beet Salad 58

Roasted Brussels Sprouts 58

Roasted Baby Potatoes 58

Roasted Sweet Potatoes 59

Roasted Pepper Salad 59

Herbed Roasted Zucchini 59

Lemon-herb Sweet Potatoes 60

Parmesan Fennel Patties 60

Buttery Roasted Carrots 60

Herb And Garlic Potatoes 61

Cheesy Butternut Squash 61

Vegan Recipes **62**

Spicy Creamed Beet Salad 62

Smoked Tempeh Sandwich 62

Roasted Golden Beets 62

Rosemary Roasted Potatoes 63

Cashew Oatmeal Muffins 63

Mediterranean-style Fingerling Potatoes 63

Italian-style Eggplant 64

Fried Broccoli Florets 64

Fried Tofu With Sweet Potatoes 64

Toasted Tortillas With Avocado 65

Classic Toasted Sandwich 65

Italian-style Cremini Mushrooms 65

Cabbage Steaks With Tofu 66

Kid-friendly Corn Muffins 66

Autumn Pumpkin Pancakes 66

Quinoa And Chickpea Meatballs 67

Carrot Puree With Herbs 67

Roasted Garlic Cabbage 67

Crispy Breaded Mushrooms 68

Authentic Indian Kofta 68

Desserts Recipes 69

Peach Crumble Cake 69

Vanilla Maple Apricots 69

Homemade Pâte à Choux 69

Vanilla And Honey-roasted Peaches 70

Almond Energy Bars 70

Fluffy Almond Brownie Squares 70

Vanilla Walnut Blondies 71

Classic Chocolate Brownie 71

Father's Day Croissants 72

Easy Vanilla Donuts 72

Favorite Chocolate Lava Cake 72

Authentic Cuban Tostada 73

Classic Cinnamon Tostada 73

Cinnamon Waffle Sticks 73

Old-fashioned Beignets 74

Grandma's Baked Apples 74

Old-fashioned Walnut Brownies 74

Key Lime Cheesecake 75

Baked Apples With Walnuts And Raisins 75

Walnut Banana Bread 76

RECIPES INDEX 77

Fundamentals of the Instant Vortex Air Fryer Oven

What Is Instant Vortex Air Fryer Oven?

The Instant Vortex Air Fryer Oven utilizes advanced technology to help people cook their favorite family foods with just one touch! It runs on a simple hot air technology which allows your food to be crispy on the outside and tender on the inside using a minimal amount of oil. The Instant Vortex Air Fryer Oven has eight cooking programs: dehydrate, air fry, roast, bake, toast, broil, reheat, and proof. The appliance blows scorching air inside the oven, and the convection fan will distribute the hot air to allow the device to cook the meal effectively. This technology will enable you to cook foods well and evenly. Further, your air fryer is equipped with a digital display that shows the cooking time and temperature and various options and buttons to select smart cooking programs.

The vortex air fryer usually releases heat from the heating element while cooking. It also has an exhaust fan located above the cooking chamber. This will allow circulating air required to cook the food and maintain fresh air circulation throughout the cooking process. Besides, it ensures that the air entering the oven is fresh and filtered to allow you to cook food more healthily. As for cooking accessories, the vortex air fryer comes with six accessories with two cooking trays, a rotisserie spit, a rotisserie basket, a drip pan, a rotisserie lift, and a rotisserie fork. You should place the ingredients in a cooking tray or rotisserie basket, press the desired button, and wait for your meal to get cooked. Thanks to the cooking trays incorporated in the Instant Vortex Air Fryer Oven, you can distribute a relatively large amount of food on them in a single layer. In this way, the heat distribution will be much more uniform than in a conventional air fryer, and you will achieve much faster and more homogeneous cooking!

Main Functions of Instant Vortex Air Fryer Oven

The cooking buttons are intuitive and guide you all along the cooking process. It tells you when to add food and when to remove it. Among them, the four cooking modes of Air Fry, Roast, Broil, and Bake have a preheating program before the cooking, while the other modes do not have a preheating program. The 8 smart cooking programs are simple to use:

Air Fry

This cooking mode is suitable for all your favorite deep-fried meals, like fries, cauliflower bites, wings, nuggets, and more. It cooks the food evenly, both fresh and frozen, with a crisp and crunchy outside and the inside tender.

Roast

This function is ideal for cooking vegetable dishes, beef, lamb, pork, poultry, etc. With this function, you will get a crisp on the outside.

Broil

Broiling is top-down direct heat, perfect for melting cheese on onion soup, machos, and more. This cooking function is used to give a final touch to the food.

Bake

This function works well for cakes, cupcakes, muffins, etc. You can bake larger quantities as you have two cooking trays.

Dehydrate

Dehydration is a slow process. It is perfect for homemade fruit leather, jerky, dried vegetables, etc. It takes several hours to dehydrate the food, but it gives a tasty flavor to the food.

Reheat

You can easily warm up your food with this function. You can reheat leftovers and save your budget with this useful function.

Proof

To get the scrumptious, loaves and rolls, allow the dough to rest and rise and let the yeast its job with this smart program!

Toast

There are no specific temperature settings in this cooking mode, only three levels of cooking temperature. The toasting level is also affected by how close you place the cooking tray to the element.

Buttons & User Guide of Instant Vortex Air Fryer Oven

The Instant Vortex Air Fryer oven has a touch screen that allows you to choose the function you want to introduce. These functions are easy to key in and are described as follows.

Display

The vortex air fryer has a digital panel that makes your cooking convenient and easy. You can select the automatic as well as the manual function. The functions are easy to key in, and you can change them until you have found the correct function you want.

Smart Programs

The programs are automated and by using them, you will not need to set temperature or cooking time. Usually, when the air fryer goes on standby mode, it indicates "OFF". The smart programs included in the oven include: Roast, Air Fry, Bake, Broil, Dehydrate, Reheat

+/- Temp

The "+" button is used to raise the temperature, and the "-" button is used to lower the temperature.

+/- Time

This is used to adjust the time taken in cooking your food. You can use the "+" to increase the time taken to cook the food or use "-" to reduce the time taken in cooking the food depending on your taste and preference.

Rotate

This is a function key that you can use while roasting or any other process that requires a rotisserie. This button is only available when you choose to roast or air fry.

Light

The Light button is used to turn ON and OFF the oven light.

Cancel

This function is vital in stopping the cooking process. This is important, especially if you have chosen the wrong function.

Start

This function is effective in beginning the cooking process.

The Benefits of Using Instant Vortex Air Fryer Oven

The Instant Vortex Air Fryer Oven, which comes in a perfect shape and size to suit all cooking needs and serving sizes, offers the following known benefits to all its users:

The Flip Feature:

Unlike other food appliances that need manual oversight for the food cooking, this appliance detects when the food needs to be flipped or tossed and then blinks the FLIP sign on its led screen, so the user knows when to flip the food. This feature ensures even cooking and reduces the risk of burning.

Six in One Multipurpose Appliance:

The smart cooking mechanism is installed to provide six different cooking functions to enable easy and effective cooking every time. The following are the smart programs of this device:

Air Fry

Roast

Broil

Bake

Reheat

Dehydrate

Go Rotisserie:

You can't really imagine cooking a whole chicken on a rotisserie without having a perfect space and a cooking appliance. With the Instant Vortex Air Fryer Oven, you can do this using its special rotisserie basket, which carries the chicken for even roasting.

Cost-Effective:

When it comes to time, energy, and money consumption, this vortex oven turns out to be extremely budget friendly. Its vortex heating system consumes lesser units of electricity in each session, thus saving the electricity expenses.

Larger Space:

The largest of the Instant Vortex Air Fryer Oven comes in a 10-quart size with three-story interior, which can practically carry all serving sizes whether you have a small family or a large one; it can cook for all.

User-Friendly Control System:

The control panels of the Instant Vortex Air Fryer Oven have been made super easy to use for all, even beginners. Each smart function is selected through a single touch, and the temperature and time can also be adjusted manually.

Breakfast Recipes

Biscuits With Smoked Sausage

Servings: 4
Cooking Time: 15 Minutes
Ingredients:

- 8 ounces refrigerated crescent dinner rolls
- 1/2 pound smoked sausage, chopped
- 1 cups cheddar cheese, shredded

Directions:

1. Select the "Air Fry" function and adjust the temperature to 350 degrees F. Press the "Start" key.
2. Meanwhile, separate the dough into 4 biscuits.
3. Unroll the crescent dough on a work surface and cut it into bite-sized pieces. Mix the crescent dough pieces with sausage and cheese. Mix to combine and roll the mixture into balls.
4. When the display indicates "Add Food", place the biscuits on a parchment-lined baking tray. Bake your biscuits for about 10 minutes.
5. Bon appétit!

Nutrition:

- Info415 Calories,23.4g Fat,32g Carbs,22.1g Protei.

Sweet Corn Muffins

Servings: 6
Cooking Time: 15 Minutes
Ingredients:

- 1 cup flour
- 1 cup yellow cornmeal
- 1/2 teaspoon salt
- 1 teaspoon baking powder
- 1 teaspoon baking soda
- 1 cup buttermilk
- 1/4 cup water
- 2 large eggs
- 1/2 cup brown sugar
- 1/4 cup butter, melted

Directions:

1. Select the "Bake" function and adjust the temperature to 330 degrees F. Press the "Start" key.
2. In a mixing bowl, stir together the dry ingredients. Then, in a separate bowl, thoroughly combine all the wet ingredients.
3. Add the wet mixture to the dry ingredients and stir just until moistened. Spoon the batter into a parchment-lined muffin tin.
4. Bake your muffins for 13 minutes or until a tester comes out dry.
5. Bon appétit!

Nutrition:

- Info315 Calories,10.2g Fat,47g Carbs,7.6g Protei.

Vegetable And Sausage Frittata

Servings: 4
Cooking Time: 20 Minutes
Ingredients:

- 1 teaspoon olive oil
- 1/2 pound cooked breakfast sausage, crumbled
- 6 eggs, beaten
- 1/2 cup cheddar cheese, shredded
- 1 chili pepper, seeded and chopped
- 1 small red onion, chopped
- 1 teaspoon garlic, pressed
- Sea salt and ground black pepper, to taste
- 1 teaspoon paprika

Directions:

1. Select the "Air Fry" function and adjust the temperature to 330 degrees F. Press the "Start" key.
2. Grease a baking pan with olive oil and set it aside.
3. In a mixing bowl, thoroughly combine all the ingredients. Pour the mixture into the prepared baking pan.
4. Bake your frittata for 15 minutes or until a tester comes out dry and clean.
5. Bon appétit!

Nutrition:

- Info367 Calories,28.6g Fat,6.4g Carbs,19.1g Protei.

Mom's Cheesy Biscuits

Servings: 6

Cooking Time: 25 Minutes

Ingredients:

- 2 cups self-rising flour
- 1 tablespoon sugar
- 1/3 cup butter
- 1/2 cup Colby cheese, grated
- 1 cup buttermilk
- 1 cup all-purpose flour, for shaping

Directions:

1. Line a baking pan with parchment paper.
2. Thoroughly combine self-rising flour and sugar. Add in butter, cheese, and buttermilk; stir to combine well.
3. Spread the all-purpose on a work surface. Then, scoop 6 balls of dough into the flour, coating them with flour and shaking off any excess flour. Place the floured dough balls in the prepared baking pan.
4. Select the "Air Fry" function and adjust the temperature to 380 degrees F. Press the "Start" key.
5. When the display indicates "Add Food", place the baking pan on the air fryer tray. Air fry for 20 minutes. Bon appétit!

Nutrition:

- Info377 Calories,14.6g Fat,50.2g Carbs,10.3g Protei.

Cheesy Egg Cups

Servings: 2

Cooking Time: 15 Minutes

Ingredients:

- 2 teaspoons olive oil
- 2 large egg
- 2 tablespoons sour cream
- 2 tablespoons cheddar cheese, grated
- Sea salt and ground black pepper, to taste

Directions:

1. Select the "Bake" function and adjust the temperature to 350 degrees F and the time to 13 minutes. Press the "Start" key.

2. Meanwhile, brush two silicone muffin cups with olive oil. Mix all the ingredients until well combined. Divide the mixture between the muffin cups.
3. When the display indicates "Add Food", place the muffin cups on the cooking tray in the center position.
4. Cook the egg cups to your desired texture, and serve warm. Enjoy!

Nutrition:

- Info277 Calories,20.2g Fat,5.8g Carbs,18.2g Protei.

Loaded Hash Browns

Servings: 4

Cooking Time: 20 Minutes

Ingredients:

- 1 tablespoon olive oil
- 16 ounces hash browns, shredded
- 1/2 pound ham, diced
- 2 garlic cloves, minced
- 1 small onion, chopped
- 1 bell pepper, seeded and diced
- 1 jalapeno pepper, seeded and chopped
- 7 eggs, whisked
- 1 cup full-fat milk
- 1 teaspoon paprika
- 1 teaspoon dried rosemary, chopped
- Sea salt and ground black pepper, to taste
- 1 cup Colby cheese, shredded

Directions:

1. Select the "Air Fry" function and adjust the temperature to 380 degrees F. Press the "Start" key.
2. Grease the sides and bottom of a casserole dish with olive oil.
3. Place the hash browns, ham, garlic, onion, and peppers in the prepared casserole dish.
4. Then, whisk the eggs, milk, and spices until everything is well incorporated. Spoon the topping over the hash browns; top with cheese.
5. When the display indicates "Add Food", place the baking pan on the air fryer tray.
6. Bake for about 15 minutes or until everything is cooked through. Bon appétit!

Nutrition:

- Info448 Calories,23.3g Fat,29.4g Carbs,31.3g Protei.

Classic Banana Beignets

Servings: 4
Cooking Time: 15 Minutes
Ingredients:

- 2 large ripe bananas
- 1 teaspoon vanilla essence
- 1/2 teaspoon cinnamon powder
- 1/2 teaspoon ground cloves
- 4 tablespoons brown sugar
- A pinch of kosher salt
- 1 cup all-purpose flour

Directions:

1. Select the "Air Fry" function and adjust the temperature to 360 degrees F. Press the "Start" key.
2. Line a baking pan with parchment paper and set it aside.
3. In a mixing bowl, thoroughly combine all the ingredients. Shape the mixture into equal balls and place them on the prepared baking pan.
4. Cook your beignets for about 10 minutes, flipping them halfway through the cooking time
5. Bon appétit!

Nutrition:

- Info205 Calories,0.5g Fat,45.7g Carbs,3.8g Protei.

Peppery Breakfast Quiche

Servings: 3
Cooking Time: 20 Minutes
Ingredients:

- 1 tablespoon olive oil
- 5 large eggs
- 1 red bell pepper, seeded and diced
- 1 green bell pepper, seeded and diced
- 2 tablespoons scallions, sliced
- 4 ounces brown mushrooms, sliced
- 1 teaspoon paprika
- Sea salt and ground black pepper, to taste
- 1/4 cup cream cheese, at room temperature

Directions:

1. Select the "Air Fry" function and adjust the temperature to 330 degrees F. Press the "Start" key.
2. Grease a baking pan with olive oil and set it aside.
3. In a mixing bowl, thoroughly combine all the ingredients. Pour the mixture into the prepared baking pan.
4. Bake your frittata for 15 minutes or until a tester comes out dry and clean.
5. Bon appétit!

Nutrition:

- Info365 Calories,19.7g Fat,34.7g Carbs,17.8g Protei.

Vanilla Pear Beignets

Servings: 4
Cooking Time: 15 Minutes
Ingredients:

- 2 large pears, cored and diced
- 2 cups all-purpose flour
- 1/2 cup brown sugar
- 2 teaspoons baking powder
- 1/2 teaspoon salt
- 1 teaspoon cinnamon powder
- 1/4 teaspoon ground cloves
- 3/4 cup apple juice
- 2 eggs
- 2 tablespoons butter, melted
- 1 teaspoon vanilla

Directions:

1. Select the "Air Fry" function and adjust the temperature to 360 degrees F. Press the "Start" key.
2. Line a baking pan with parchment paper and set it aside.
3. In a mixing bowl, thoroughly combine all the ingredients. Shape the mixture into equal balls and place them on the prepared baking pan.
4. Cook your beignets for about 10 minutes, flipping them halfway through the cooking time. Dust your beignets with confectioners' sugar, if desired.
5. Bon appétit!

Nutrition:

- Info450 Calories,8.6g Fat,83.7g Carbs,9.7g Protei.

Scotch Eggs With Sausage

Servings: 4
Cooking Time: 25 Minutes
Ingredients:
- 4 medium eggs
- 1/2 cup all-purpose flour
- 1/2 cup tortilla chips, crushed
- Sea salt and ground black pepper, to taste
- 8 ounces breakfast sausage

Directions:
1. Place the eggs in a small saucepan and cover them with cold water. Bring to a boil; remove from the heat, cover, and let them sit for 3 minutes. Next, fill the saucepan with cold water to cool the eggs.
2. After that, carefully peel the eggs under cold running water. Keep the eggs chilled.
3. Mix the flour, crushed corn tortillas, salt, and black pepper in a shallow bowl. Divide the sausage into 4 equal portions and form them into thin patties. Place 1 boiled egg on top of each sausage patty and wrap them around the boiled eggs.
4. Select the "Broil" function and adjust the temperature to 400 degrees F. Press the "Start" key.
5. When the display indicates "Add Food", place the eggs on the cooking tray. Cook your scotch eggs for 20 minutes.
6. Serve immediately and enjoy!

Nutrition:
- Info333 Calories,22.4g Fat,15.6g Carbs,15.6g Protei.

Favorite Pizza Sandwich

Servings: 2
Cooking Time: 10 Minutes
Ingredients:
- 4 slices bread
- 2 tablespoons tomato paste
- 4 slices mozzarella cheese
- 16 slices pepperoni

Directions:
1. Assemble two sandwiches with the bread slices, tomato paste, cheese, and pepperoni; you can use a toothpick to keep the sandwich together.
2. Select the "Toast" function and press the "Start" key.
3. When the display indicates "Add Food", place the sandwich on the air fryer tray.
4. Toast the sandwich for about 3 minutes or so. Bon appétit!

Nutrition:
- Info357 Calories,17.9g Fat,24.3g Carbs,23.3g Protei.

Grandma's Apple Fritters

Servings: 4
Cooking Time: 15 Minutes
Ingredients:
- 1/4 cup plus 1 teaspoon coconut oil, melted
- 1 cup all-purpose flour
- 1/4 cup brown sugar
- 1 teaspoon baking powder
- 1 teaspoon ground cinnamon
- 1/2 teaspoon ground cloves
- 1/4 teaspoon kosher salt
- 1/2 cup full-fat milk
- 2 eggs, whisked
- 1 teaspoon vanilla paste (or extract)
- 2 medium apples, peeled and grated
- 1 cup confectioners' sugar

Directions:
1. Select the "Air Fry" function and adjust the temperature to 360 degrees F. Press the "Start" key.
2. Grease a baking pan with 1 teaspoon of coconut oil and set it aside.
3. In a mixing bowl, thoroughly combine the flour, brown sugar, baking powder, spices, milk, eggs, vanilla, apples, and 1/4 cup of coconut oil. Shape the mixture into equal patties and place them on the prepared baking pan.
4. Cook your fritters for about 10 minutes, flipping them halfway through the cooking time. Dust your fritters with confectioners' sugar.
5. Bon appétit!

Nutrition:
- Info451 Calories,16.3g Fat,69.6g Carbs,7.2g Protei.

Baked Pita Bread

Servings: 2
Cooking Time: 10 Minutes
Ingredients:
- 2 pita breads
- 1 teaspoon Dijon mustard
- 2 ounces mozzarella cheese slices
- 1/2 teaspoon dried oregano
- 1 medium tomato, sliced
- 2 ounces Kalamata olives, pitted and sliced

Directions:
1. Assemble pita breads with the other ingredients; you can use a toothpick to secure your pitas.
2. Select the "Toast" function and press the "Start" key.
3. When the display indicates "Add Food", place the sandwich on the air fryer tray.
4. Toast the sandwich for about 3 minutes. Enjoy!

Nutrition:
- Info289 Calories,10.1g Fat,36g Carbs,13.7g Protei.

Traditional Polish Naleśniki

Servings: 4
Cooking Time: 15 Minutes
Ingredients:
- 1 cup all-purpose flour
- 1/2 teaspoon granulated sugar
- 1/2 teaspoon salt
- 1 cup milk
- 2 large eggs, whisked
- 2 tablespoons butter, melted
- 4 ounces cottage cheese
- 1/2 cup raisins, soaked for 15 minutes

Directions:
1. In a mixing bowl, thoroughly combine the flour, sugar, and salt. Gradually add in the milk, eggs, and butter; mix to combine well.

2. Grease a baking pan with nonstick cooking oil and set it aside.
3. Select the "Air Fry" function and adjust the temperature to 350 degrees F. Press the "Start" key.
4. When the display indicates "Add Food", place the nalesniki on the cooking tray in the center position.
5. Cook your nalesniki for about 13 minutes, working in batches, if needed. Enjoy!

Nutrition:
- Info268 Calories,11.6g Fat,28.2g Carbs,11.5g Protei.

Traditional Greek Tiganites

Servings: 5
Cooking Time: 15 Minutes
Ingredients:
- 1 ½ cups all-purpose flour
- 1 teaspoon baking powder
- 1/2 baking soda
- 1/2 teaspoon kosher salt
- 1 teaspoon granulated sugar
- 1 cup lukewarm water
- 1/2 cup Greek-style yogurt
- 1 large egg, whisked
- Topping:
- 1/2 cup honey

Directions:
1. In a mixing bowl, thoroughly combine the dry ingredients. In another bowl, whisk the wet ingredients. Add the wet mixture to the dry ingredients, and mix to combine well.
2. Grease a baking pan with nonstick cooking oil and set it aside.
3. Select the "Air Fry" function and adjust the temperature to 350 degrees F. Press the "Start" key.
4. Cook your tiganites for about 13 minutes or until they turn golden brown; work in batches, if needed. Enjoy!

Nutrition:
- Info222 Calories,1.3g Fat,47.3g Carbs,5.2g Protei.

Mustard Cheese Sandwich

Servings: 2
Cooking Time: 10 Minutes
Ingredients:

- 4 large slices crusty bread
- 2 teaspoons Dijon mustard
- 4 ounces Colby cheese, thinly sliced
- 2 tablespoons chives, roughly chopped

Directions:

1. Assemble your sandwich with mustard, cheese, and chives; you can use a toothpick to keep the sandwich together.
2. Select the "Toast" function and press the "Start" key.
3. When the display indicates "Add Food", place the sandwich on the air fryer tray.
4. Toast the sandwich for about 3 minutes. Serve immediately.

Nutrition:

- Info385 Calories,20.4g Fat,31.5g Carbs,19.1g Protei.

Mediterranean-style Cornbread Muffins

Servings: 6
Cooking Time: 15 Minutes
Ingredients:

- 1 cup yellow cornmeal
- 1 cup all-purpose flour
- 1 tablespoon honey
- 1 teaspoon baking powder
- 1 teaspoon baking soda
- 1/2 teaspoon kosher salt
- 1 cup buttermilk
- 1/2 cup water
- 2 eggs, beaten
- 2 tablespoons olives, pitted and sliced
- 6 tablespoons extra-virgin olive oil

Directions:

1. Select the "Bake" function and adjust the temperature to 330 degrees F. Press the "Start" key.
2. In a mixing bowl, stir together the dry ingredients. Then, in a separate bowl, thoroughly combine all the wet ingredients.
3. Add the wet mixture to the dry ingredients and stir just until moistened. Fold in the olives. Spoon the batter into a parchment-lined muffin tin.
4. Bake your muffins for 13 minutes or until a tester comes out dry.
5. Bon appétit!

Nutrition:

- Info348 Calories,16.7g Fat,41.8g Carbs,7.3g Protei.

Fall Pumpkin Pancakes

Servings: 4
Cooking Time: 15 Minutes
Ingredients:

- 1 teaspoon coconut oil
- 1 cup pumpkin puree
- 1/2 cup brown sugar
- 2/3 cup peanut butter
- 2 eggs
- 1 teaspoon pumpkin pie spice
- 1 teaspoon baking powder

Directions:

1. Grease a baking pan with coconut oil and set it aside.
2. In a mixing bowl, thoroughly combine all the ingredients; mix to combine well.
3. Select the "Air Fry" function and adjust the temperature to 350 degrees F. Press the "Start" key. Spoon your pancakes onto the baking pan.
4. When the display indicates "Add Food", place the baking pan on the air fryer tray.
5. Cook your pancakes for about 13 minutes, working in batches, if needed.
6. Bon appétit!

Nutrition:

- Info440 Calories,25.5g Fat,42.3g Carbs,14.7g Protei.

Classic Breakfast Frittata

Servings: 4

Cooking Time: 20 Minutes

Ingredients:

- 1 tablespoon olive oil
- 6 eggs
- 1 shallot, peeled and chopped
- 6 tablespoons sour cream
- 1 cup Monetary-Jack cheese, shredded
- 1/2 teaspoon cayenne pepper
- Coarse sea salt and ground black pepper, to taste

Directions:

1. Select the "Air Fry" function and adjust the temperature to 330 degrees F. Press the "Start" key.
2. Grease a baking pan with nonstick cooking oil and set it aside.
3. In a mixing bowl, thoroughly combine all the ingredients. Pour the mixture into the prepared baking pan.
4. Bake your frittata for 15 minutes or until a tester comes out dry and clean.
5. Bon appétit!

Nutrition:

- Info265 Calories,20.5g Fat,3.8g Carbs,16.1g Protei.

Greek-style Pita Pizza

Servings: 2

Cooking Time: 10 Minutes

Ingredients:

- 1 teaspoon olive oil
- 2 medium pita breads
- 4 tablespoons tomato sauce
- 4 ounces feta cheese, crumbled
- 1 tablespoon Greek seasoning mix

Directions:

1. Select the "Air Fry" function and adjust the temperature to 390 degrees F. Press the "Start" key.
2. Then, grease the cooking tray with olive oil.
3. Top your pita with tomato sauce, cheese, and seasoning mix.
4. Bake your pizza for about 5 minutes or until the cheese is melted. Bon appétit!

Nutrition:

- Info300 Calories,15.3g Fat,26.6g Carbs,11.7g Protei.

Appetizers And Snacks Recipes

The Best Cheese Broccomole

Servings: 7
Cooking Time: 15 Minutes
Ingredients:
- 1 pound broccoli florets
- 2 teaspoons olive oil
- 6 ounces feta cheese, crumbled
- 1/4 cup cream of onion soup
- 1 teaspoon cayenne pepper
- 1 teaspoon garlic powder
- Kosher salt and freshly ground black pepper, to taste
- 1/2 cup Parmesan cheese, grated

Directions:
1. Toss the broccoli florets with olive oil.
2. Select the "Air Fry" function and adjust the temperature to 400 degrees F. Press the "Start" key.
3. Arrange the broccoli florets on the air fryer oven perforated pan, making sure not to crowd them.
4. Air fry the broccoli florets for 6 minutes or until cooked through, tossing them once or twice during the cooking time.
5. Blend the roasted broccoli with feta cheese, onion soup, and spices until creamy and uniform. Spoon the sauce into a lightly greased casserole dish.
6. Top the sauce with parmesan cheese and select the "Broil" function. Broil the sauce until the cheese melts.
7. Bon appétit!

Nutrition:
- Info134 Calories,8.9g Fat,7.2g Carbs,7.5g Protei.

Smoky Carrot Dip

Servings: 7
Cooking Time: 25 Minutes
Ingredients:
- 1 ½ pounds carrots, trimmed and sliced
- 3 teaspoons olive oil
- 2 cloves garlic, minced
- 1 teaspoon lime zest
- 1 teaspoon lemon juice
- 1 teaspoon Dijon mustard
- Sea salt and ground black pepper, to taste
- 1/4 cup tahini
- 1/2 teaspoon ground cumin
- 1/2 teaspoon turmeric powder

Directions:
1. Toss the carrots with olive oil in a mixing bowl.
2. Select the "Air Fry" function and adjust the temperature to 380 degrees F. Press the "Start" key.
3. Arrange your carrots on the parchment-lined air fryer oven perforated pan.
4. Air fry your carrots for 20 minutes or until tender and cooked through. Blend the carrots with the remaining ingredients until creamy and uniform.
5. Bon appétit!

Nutrition:
- Info113 Calories,6.8g Fat,12.4g Carbs,2.6g Protei.

Honey Apple Chips

Servings: 4
Cooking Time: 35 Minutes
Ingredients:
- 2 medium apples, cored and sliced
- 1 tablespoon coconut oil, melted
- 2 tablespoons honey
- 1/4 teaspoon grated nutmeg
- 1 teaspoon ground cinnamon

Directions:
1. Select the "Air Fry" function and adjust the temperature to 300 degrees F. Press the "Start" key.
2. Toss your apples with the remaining ingredients. Place a sheet of parchment paper in the air fryer oven pan.
3. Air fry the apple slices for 15 minutes; turn them over and continue to cook for a further 15 minutes or until they are golden-browned.
4. Bon appétit!

Nutrition:

- Info112 Calories,3.6g Fat,21.4g Carbs,0.5g Protei.

Savory Herb Walnuts

Servings: 9

Cooking Time: 20 Minutes

Ingredients:

- 2 cups raw walnuts
- 2 tablespoons olive oil
- 1 teaspoon dried thyme
- 1 teaspoon dried rosemary
- 2 tablespoons nutritional yeast
- Sea salt and cayenne pepper, to taste

Directions:

1. Select the "Air Fry" function and adjust the temperature to 320 degrees F. Press the "Start" key.
2. Toss all the ingredients on the parchment-lined air fryer oven perforated pan.
3. Air fry the walnuts for 15 minutes or until the walnuts turn golden-brown.
4. Enjoy!

Nutrition:

- Info181 Calories,17.5g Fat,4.4g Carbs,4.5g Protei.

Cheesy Broccoli Tots

Servings: 4

Cooking Time: 15 Minutes

Ingredients:

- 1 pound broccoli, grated
- 1/2 cup cheddar cheese, shredded
- 1 tablespoon extra-virgin olive oil
- 1 egg
- 1/2 cup panko breadcrumbs
- 2 cloves garlic, minced
- Sea salt and freshly ground black pepper, to taste

Directions:

1. Select the "Air Fry" function and adjust the temperature to 390 degrees F. Press the "Start" key.
2. Place a sheet of parchment paper in the air fryer oven pan. Thoroughly combine all the ingredients.

3. Form the mixture into equal balls and place them in a single layer in the air fryer oven perforated pan.
4. Air fry the broccoli tots for 10 minutes, turning them over halfway through.
5. Bon appétit!

Nutrition:

- Info145 Calories,9.9g Fat,6.7g Carbs,8.9g Protei.

Classic Parsnip Fries

Servings: 4

Cooking Time: 20 Minutes

Ingredients:

- 1 pound parsnip, cut into matchsticks
- 2 teaspoons extra-virgin olive oil
- 1/2 teaspoon garlic powder
- 1/2 teaspoon smoked paprika
- Kosher salt and ground black pepper, to taste

Directions:

1. Toss the parsnip with the remaining ingredients.
2. Select the "Air Fry" function and adjust the temperature to 390 degrees F. Press the "Start" key.
3. Arrange the parsnip sticks on the parchment-lined air fryer oven perforated pan.
4. Air fry the parsnip sticks for 15 minutes or until golden-brown and crisp.
5. Bon appétit!

Nutrition:

- Info113 Calories,2.6g Fat,21.6g Carbs,1.6g Protei.

Peppery Bean Dip

Servings: 9
Cooking Time: 20 Minutes
Ingredients:

- 4 bell peppers
- 2 teaspoon olive oil
- 1 cup canned or boiled red beans
- 2 tablespoons fresh basil leaves
- 2 tablespoons fresh parsley leaves
- 1 tablespoon fresh mint leaves
- 4 tablespoons Pecorino cheese, grated
- 1 tablespoon freshly squeezed lemon juice
- 2 garlic cloves, peeled and chopped
- Kosher salt and ground black pepper, to taste
- 1/4 cup tahini

Directions:

1. Toss the bell peppers with olive oil.
2. Select the "Air Fry" function and adjust the temperature to 400 degrees F. Press the "Start" key.
3. Arrange the peppers on the air fryer oven perforated pan.
4. Air fry the peppers for 15 minutes or until they're browned, shaking the pan once or twice during cooking.
5. Place the roasted peppers along with the remaining ingredients in a bowl of your food processor. Blend the mixture until creamy and uniform.
6. Bon appétit!

Nutrition:

- Info119 Calories,6.3g Fat,12.6g Carbs,4.9g Protei.

Restaurant-style Onion Rings

Servings: 4
Cooking Time: 15 Minutes
Ingredients:

- 1 large onion, peeled and sliced
- 1 cup seasoned breadcrumbs
- 1/2 cup mayonnaise
- 1 teaspoon cumin powder
- 1/2 teaspoon mustard powder
- Kosher salt and ground black pepper, to taste

Directions:

1. Toss the onion rings with the other ingredients.
2. Select the "Air Fry" function and adjust the temperature to 390 degrees F. Press the "Start" key.
3. Arrange the onion rings on the parchment-lined air fryer oven perforated pan.
4. Air fry the onion rings for 10 minutes or until golden brown. Enjoy!

Nutrition:

- Info314 Calories,20.7g Fat,23.4g Carbs,2.3g Protei.

Montreal Chicken Drumettes

Servings: 6
Cooking Time: 25 Minutes
Ingredients:

- 2 pounds chicken drumettes
- 1 cup tomato sauce
- 2 tablespoons olive oil
- 1 teaspoon Montreal seasoning mix
- 1 tablespoon fresh basil, chopped
- 1 tablespoon fresh parsley, chopped
- 1 tablespoon fresh cilantro, chopped

Directions:

1. Select the "Air Fry" function and adjust the temperature to 375 degrees F. Press the "Start" key.
2. Place a sheet of parchment paper in the air fryer oven pan. Toss the chicken wings with the remaining ingredients.
3. Arrange the chicken wings in a single layer in the air fryer oven perforated pan.
4. Air fry the chicken wings for 10 minutes; turn them over and air fry for a further 10 minutes or until they are browned and crunchy.
5. Bon appétit!

Nutrition:

- Info257 Calories,8.7g Fat,9.4g Carbs,31.9g Protei.

Cheese Broccoli Dip

Servings: 8
Cooking Time: 15 Minutes
Ingredients:

- 1 pound broccoli florets
- 2 teaspoon olive oil
- 2 scallion stalks, chopped
- 1 garlic clove, minced
- 1/4 cup cilantro leaves, chopped
- 1 lime, squeezed
- Sea salt and ground black pepper, to taste
- 1/4 cup cream cheese

Directions:

1. Toss the broccoli florets with olive oil.
2. Select the "Air Fry" function and adjust the temperature to 400 degrees F. Press the "Start" key.
3. Arrange the broccoli florets on the air fryer oven perforated pan, making sure not to crowd them.
4. Air fry the broccoli florets for 6 minutes or until cooked through, tossing them once or twice during the cooking time.
5. Blend the roasted broccoli with the remaining ingredients until creamy and uniform.
6. Bon appétit!

Nutrition:

- Info69 Calories,3.9g Fat,3.7g Carbs,3.5g Protei.

Cheese Prawn Wontons

Servings: 4
Cooking Time: 15 Minutes
Ingredients:

- 6 ounces shrimp, peeled, deveined and chopped
- 4 ounces cream cheese, at room temperature
- 2 teaspoons sesame oil
- 2 tablespoons green olive, chopped
- 2 cloves garlic, minced
- 1 teaspoon Sriracha, optional
- Sea salt and ground black pepper, to taste
- 16 wonton wrappers
- 1 extra-large egg, well beaten with 1 tablespoon of water

Directions:

1. In a mixing bowl, thoroughly combine all the ingredients, except the wonton wrappers.
2. Divide the mixture between the wonton wrappers.
3. Fold each wonton in half. Bring up the 2 ends of the wonton and use the egg wash to stick them together. Pinch the edges and coat each wonton with egg wash.
4. Place the folded wontons on the air fryer oven perforated pan, making sure not to crowd them.
5. Select the "Air Fry" function and adjust the temperature to 380 degrees F. Press the "Start" key.
6. Air fry your wontons for 10 minutes or until they're lightly browned.
7. Bon appétit!

Nutrition:

- Info277 Calories,14.3g Fat,21.4g Carbs,15.6g Protei.

Italian Cheese Sticks

Servings: 6
Cooking Time: 10 Minutes
Ingredients:

- 2 medium eggs
- 1 teaspoon Italian seasoning
- 1 cup Italian breadcrumbs
- 6 mozzarella sticks

Directions:

1. Select the "Air Fry" function and adjust the temperature to 390 degrees F. Press the "Start" key.
2. Place a sheet of parchment paper in the air fryer oven pan.
3. Whisk the eggs in a mixing bowl; then, add in the seasoning and breadcrumbs and mix to combine well.
4. Dip each mozzarella stick into the egg mixture.
5. Air fry your mozzarella sticks for 5 minutes; turn them over and continue to cook for a further 2 minutes or until they are golden brown and crispy.
6. Bon appétit!

Nutrition:

- Info118 Calories,6.4g Fat,5.3g Carbs,8.7g Protei.

Sausage Wonton Wraps

Servings: 6
Cooking Time: 15 Minutes
Ingredients:
- 1 pound smoked sausage, crumbled
- 2 scallion stalks, chopped
- 2 tablespoons fish sauce
- 1 teaspoon ginger-garlic paste
- 1 package wonton wrappers
- 1 egg
- 1 tablespoon olive oil

Directions:
1. In a mixing bowl, thoroughly combine crumbled sausage, scallions, fish sauce, and ginger-garlic paste.
2. Divide the mixture between wonton wrappers.
3. Whisk the egg with 1 tablespoon of olive oil and 1 tablespoon of water.
4. Fold the wonton in half. Bring up the 2 ends of the wonton and use the egg wash to stick them together. Pinch the edges and coat each wonton with egg wash.
5. Place the folded wontons on the air fryer oven perforated pan, making sure not to crowd them.
6. Select the "Air Fry" function and adjust the temperature to 380 degrees F. Press the "Start" key.
7. Air fry your wontons for 10 minutes or until they're lightly browned.
8. Bon appétit!

Nutrition:
- Info188 Calories,10.3g Fat,9g Carbs,14.6g Protei.

Favorite Cauliflower Tots

Servings: 5
Cooking Time: 15 Minutes
Ingredients:
- 1 pound cauliflower, grated
- 1 cup Mexican cheese blend, shredded
- 1/2 cup all-purpose flour
- 1 teaspoon baking powder
- 1 tablespoon butter, at room temperature
- 2 eggs, whisked
- 2 scallion stalks, chopped
- 1 cup tortilla chips, crushed
- 1/2 teaspoon cayenne pepper
- Kosher salt and ground black pepper, to taste

Directions:
1. Select the "Air Fry" function and adjust the temperature to 390 degrees F. Press the "Start" key.
2. Place a sheet of parchment paper in the air fryer oven pan. Thoroughly combine all the ingredients.
3. Form the mixture into equal balls and place them in a single layer in the air fryer oven perforated pan.
4. Air fry the cauliflower tots for 10 minutes, turning them over halfway through.
5. Bon appétit!

Nutrition:
- Info353 Calories,17.3g Fat,37.2g Carbs,13.1g Protei.

Red Beetroot Chips

Servings: 2
Cooking Time: 10 Minutes
Ingredients:
- 2 medium-size red beets, peeled and sliced
- 2 teaspoons olive oil
- 1/2 teaspoon mustard powder
- 1 teaspoon cayenne pepper
- Kosher salt and freshly ground black pepper, to taste

Directions:
1. Select the "Air Fry" function and adjust the temperature to 380 degrees F. Press the "Start" key.
2. Toss all the ingredients on the parchment-lined air fryer oven perforated pan.
3. Air fry the beetroot chips for 6 minutes or until crispy.
4. Enjoy!

Nutrition:
- Info79 Calories,4.8g Fat,8.4g Carbs,1.4g Protei.

Kid-friendly Cheese Bites

Servings: 5
Cooking Time: 15 Minutes
Ingredients:

- 2 eggs
- 1/3 cup almond flour
- 1/4 cup parmesan cheese grated
- 3 tablespoons mayonnaise
- 1 teaspoon cayenne pepper
- 1/2 teaspoon garlic powder
- 1 teaspoon Italian seasoning mix
- 5 cheese sticks

Directions:

1. Select the "Air Fry" function and adjust the temperature to 390 degrees F. Press the "Start" key.
2. Place a sheet of parchment paper in the air fryer oven pan.
3. Whisk the eggs in a mixing bowl; then, add in the almond flour, cheese, mayonnaise, and seasoning; mix to combine well.
4. Dip each cheese stick into the egg/flour mixture.
5. Air fry the cheese sticks for 5 minutes; turn them over and continue to cook for a further 2 minutes or until they are golden brown and crispy.
6. Bon appétit!

Nutrition:

- Info258 Calories,21.4g Fat,3.4g Carbs,11.9g Protei.

Garlicky Broccoli Florets

Servings: 4
Cooking Time: 10 Minutes
Ingredients:

- 1 pound broccoli florets
- 2 garlic cloves, crushed
- 1 teaspoon red pepper flakes
- 2 tablespoons olive oil
- Sea salt and ground black pepper, to taste

Directions:

1. Toss all the ingredients in a mixing bowl.

2. Select the "Air Fry" function and adjust the temperature to 400 degrees F. Press the "Start" key.
3. Arrange the broccoli florets on the air fryer oven perforated pan, making sure not to crowd them.
4. Air fry the broccoli florets for 6 minutes or until cooked through, tossing them once or twice during the cooking time.
5. Bon appétit!

Nutrition:

- Info108 Calories,7.2g Fat,8.1g Carbs,3g Protei.

Traditional Japanese Korokke

Servings: 5
Cooking Time: 15 Minutes
Ingredients:

- 1 pound mashed potatoes
- Kosher salt and ground black pepper, to taste
- 3 ounces ham, chopped
- 1 cup cheese, shredded
- 1 cup flour
- 4 eggs, whisked
- 1 cup breadcrumbs
- 2 teaspoons olive oil

Directions:

1. Select the "Air Fry" function and adjust the temperature to 390 degrees F. Press the "Start" key.
2. Place a sheet of parchment paper in the air fryer oven pan. Thoroughly combine all the ingredients.
3. Form the mixture into equal balls and place them in a single layer in the air fryer oven perforated pan.
4. Air fry the croquettes for 10 minutes, turning them over halfway through.
5. Bon appétit!

Nutrition:

- Info385 Calories,14.4g Fat,44.4g Carbs,19.2g Protei.

Brussel Sprout Chips

Servings: 2
Cooking Time: 10 Minutes
Ingredients:

- 2 cups Brussel sprouts, trimmed and separated into leaves
- 2 teaspoons olive oil
- Coarse salt and red pepper flakes, to taste
- 1/2 teaspoon smoked paprika
- 1/2 teaspoon turmeric powder

Directions:

1. Select the "Air Fry" function and adjust the temperature to 380 degrees F. Press the "Start" key.
2. Toss all the ingredients on the parchment-lined air fryer oven perforated pan.
3. Air fry the Brussel sprouts for 6 minutes or until crispy.
4. Enjoy!

Nutrition:

- Info91 Calories,4.9g Fat,10.9g Carbs,3.4g Protei.

Texas-style Fried Pickles

Servings: 4
Cooking Time: 15 Minutes
Ingredients:

- 1 large egg, beaten
- 1/2 cup all-purpose flour
- 1/2 teaspoon onion powder
- 1 teaspoon garlic powder
- Sea salt and freshly cracked black pepper, to season
- 2 large dill pickles, sliced into rounds

Directions:

1. Whisk the eggs in a shallow bowl; add in the flour and spices; mix to combine. Dredge your pickles into the egg mixture.
2. Select the "Air Fry" function and adjust the temperature to 390 degrees F. Press the "Start" key.
3. Arrange the pickle chip on the parchment-lined air fryer oven perforated pan.
4. Air fry the pickle chip for 6 minutes or until crispy and cooked through. Work in batches, if needed. Enjoy!

Nutrition:

- Info93 Calories,1.6g Fat,15.5g Carbs,3.9g Protei.

Pork And Beef Recipes

Authentic Kansas City Strip

Servings: 4
Cooking Time: 20 Minutes
Ingredients:

- 1 ½ pounds Kansas City strip steak
- 1 teaspoon Kansas City dry rub
- Kosher salt and ground black pepper, to taste
- 2 teaspoons olive oil

Directions:

1. Toss the steaks with the other ingredients.
2. Select the "Air Fry" function and adjust the temperature to 380 degrees F. Press the "Start" key. Place aluminum foil onto the drip pan.
3. When the display indicates "Add Food", place the beef in the air fryer oven perforated pan. Cook the beef for about 10 minutes.
4. Increase the temperature of the oven to 400 degrees F and continue to cook for 5 minutes more.
5. Serve warm and enjoy!

Nutrition:

- Info407 Calories,27.6g Fat,1.4g Carbs,35.3g Protei.

Roasted Boston Butt

Servings: 6
Cooking Time: 45 Minutes
Ingredients:

- 2 pounds Boston butt
- 1 tablespoon Dijon mustard
- 1 teaspoon ancho chile powder
- 2 tablespoons white vinegar
- Sea salt and ground black pepper, to taste
- 1 tablespoon smoked paprika
- 1/2 teaspoon ground cumin
- 1/2 teaspoon dried oregano
- 2 tablespoons brown sugar

Directions:

1. Add all the ingredients to a ceramic or glass bowl. Allow the pork to marinate for at least 3 hours.
2. Select the "Air Fry" function and adjust the temperature to 390 degrees F. Press the "Start" key. Place aluminum foil onto the drip pan.
3. When the display indicates "Add Food", place the pork in the air fryer oven perforated pan. Reserve the marinade. Cook the pork for about 25 minutes.
4. Baste the pork with the reserved marinade and continue to roast for about 20 minutes or until cooked through. Serve warm and enjoy!

Nutrition:

- Info362 Calories,22.7g Fat,5.3g Carbs,32.1g Protei.

Italian-style Pulled Pork

Servings: 5
Cooking Time: 55 Minutes + Marinating Time
Ingredients:

- 2 pounds boneless pork shoulder
- 1 tablespoon Italian seasoning mix
- 1/2 teaspoon cumin seeds
- 2 garlic cloves, pressed
- Sea salt and ground black pepper, to taste
- 1 teaspoon hot paprika

Directions:

1. Add all the ingredients to a ceramic or glass bowl. Allow the pork to marinate for at least 3 hours.
2. Select the "Air Fry" function and adjust the temperature to 360 degrees F. Press the "Start" key. Place aluminum foil onto the drip pan.
3. When the display indicates "Add Food", place the pork in the air fryer oven perforated pan. Reserve the marinade. Cook the pork for about 25 minutes.
4. Baste the pork with the reserved marinade and continue to roast for about 25 minutes or until cooked through. Shred the pork with two forks and serve immediately.
5. Bon appétit!

Nutrition:
- Info346 Calories,22.5g Fat,1.4g Carbs,31.8g Protei.

Orange Chuck Roast With Baby Potatoes

Servings: 5
Cooking Time: 35 Minutes
Ingredients:
- 1 ½ pounds beef chuck roast
- 2 tablespoons sesame oil
- 1 teaspoon garlic, pressed
- 1/2 cup orange juice
- 2 tablespoons Worcestershire sauce
- 1/2 teaspoon ground bay leaf
- 1 teaspoon dried oregano
- 1 teaspoon mustard
- 1 teaspoon cayenne pepper
- Sea salt and ground black pepper, to taste
- 1 pound baby potatoes, scrubbed

Directions:
1. Place the beef, sesame oil, garlic, orange juice, Worcestershire sauce, ground bay leaf, oregano, mustard, cayenne pepper, salt, and black pepper in a ceramic or glass bowl. Allow the beef to marinate for at least 3 hours.
2. Select the "Air Fry" function and adjust the temperature to 390 degrees F. Press the "Start" key. Place aluminum foil onto the drip pan.
3. When the display indicates "Add Food", place the beef in the air fryer oven perforated pan. Reserve the marinade. Cook the beef for about 15 minutes.
4. Add in baby potatoes, baste the beef with the reserved marinade, and continue to cook for 15 minutes more.
5. Serve warm and enjoy!

Nutrition:
- Info417 Calories,24.6g Fat,21.5g Carbs,28.3g Protei.

Breaded Filet Mignon

Servings: 5
Cooking Time: 15 Minutes
Ingredients:
- 1 ½ pounds filet mignon

- 1 medium egg
- 1 cup bread crumbs
- 1 tablespoon olive oil
- 1 teaspoon garlic powder
- 1 teaspoon onion powder
- 1 teaspoon mustard powder
- 1 teaspoon cayenne pepper
- Sea salt and ground black pepper, to taste

Directions:
1. Select the "Roast" function and adjust the temperature to 365 degrees F. Press the "Start" key.
2. Whisk the egg in a shallow bowl; in another shallow bowl, mix the remaining ingredients.
3. Dip the filet mignon into the whisked egg. Roll it into the crumb mixture.
4. When the display indicates "Add Food", place the beef in the air fryer oven perforated pan. Cook the beef for about 12 minutes.
5. Serve warm and enjoy!

Nutrition:
- Info255 Calories,10.2g Fat,5.5g Carbs,32.9g Protei.

Jamaican-style Pork

Servings: 4
Cooking Time: 25 Minutes + Marinating Time
Ingredients:
- 1 pound pork butt, sliced
- 2 tablespoons olive oil
- 2 Scotch bonnet peppers, chopped
- 1/4 cup apple cider vinegar
- 2 tablespoons soy sauce
- 2 tablespoons brown sugar
- 1 teaspoon allspice
- 1 teaspoon cinnamon

Directions:
1. Add all the ingredients to a ceramic or glass bowl. Allow the pork to marinate for at least 3 hours.
2. Select the "Air Fry" function and adjust the temperature to 390 degrees F. Press the "Start" key. Place aluminum foil onto the drip pan.

3. When the display indicates "Add Food", place the pork in the air fryer oven perforated pan. Reserve the marinade. Cook the pork for about 10 minutes.

4. Baste the pork with the reserved marinade and continue to roast for about 10 minutes or until cooked through. Serve immediately and enjoy!

Nutrition:
- Info386 Calories,28.6g Fat,9.1g Carbs,20.5g Protei.

Classic Homemade Cheeseburgers

Servings: 4
Cooking Time: 30 Minutes
Ingredients:
- 1 pound ground beef
- 1 teaspoon fish sauce
- 1 teaspoon liquid smoke
- 1 small onion, minced
- 1 teaspoon garlic, minced
- Kosher salt and ground black pepper, to taste
- 4 hamburger buns
- 4 slices cheddar cheese
- 4 large lettuce leaves
- 4 teaspoons Dijon mustard

Directions:
1. Select the "Air Fry" function and adjust the temperature to 390 degrees F. Press the "Start" key.
2. Place a sheet of parchment paper in the air fryer oven pan.
3. Mix the ground beef, fish sauce, liquid smoke, onion, garlic, salt, and black pepper until everything is well incorporated.
4. Shape the mixture into four patties and place them in a single layer in the air fryer oven perforated pan.
5. Air fry your cheeseburgers for 25 minutes. Assemble your cheeseburgers with warm patties, hamburger buns, cheese, lettuce, and mustard.
6. Bon appétit!

Nutrition:
- Info491 Calories,23.8g Fat,25.1g Carbs,41.3g Protei.

Traditional Greek Keftedes

Servings: 4
Cooking Time: 25 Minutes
Ingredients:
- 1/2 pound ground chuck
- 1/2 pound smoked beef sausage, crumbled
- 1 small onion, grated
- 2 garlic cloves, minced
- 2 tablespoons olive oil
- 2 medium eggs, chopped
- 2 tablespoons fresh parsley leaves, chopped
- 2 tablespoons fresh mint leaves, chopped
- 1 teaspoon dried Greek oregano
- Sea salt and ground black pepper, to taste

Directions:
1. Select the "Air Fry" function and adjust the temperature to 390 degrees F. Press the "Start" key.
2. Place a sheet of parchment paper in the air fryer oven pan. Thoroughly combine all the ingredients in a mixing bowl.
3. Form the mixture into 8 balls and place them in a single layer in the air fryer oven perforated pan; press each ball slightly using a fork.
4. Air fry your keftedes for 20 minutes. Bon appétit!

Nutrition:
- Info366 Calories,28.4g Fat,4.8g Carbs,22.5g Protei.

Pork And Sausage Patties

Servings: 4
Cooking Time: 20 Minutes
Ingredients:
- 1/2 pound ground pork
- 1/2 pound turkey sausage, crumbled
- 1 small onion, chopped
- 2 garlic cloves, minced
- 1 cup crackers, crushed
- 2 large eggs, beaten
- Kosher salt and ground black pepper, to taste
- 2 tablespoons olive oil

Directions:

1. Thoroughly combine all the ingredients in a mixing bowl. Shape the mixture into four patties.
2. Select the "Air Fry" function and adjust the temperature to 370 degrees F. Press the "Start" key. Place aluminum foil onto the drip pan.
3. When the display indicates "Add Food", place the pork burgers in the air fryer oven perforated pan. Cook your burgers for about 8 minutes.
4. Flip the burgers over and continue to cook them for a further 8 minutes.
5. Bon appétit!

Nutrition:

- Info369 Calories,27.3g Fat,2.8g Carbs,26.7g Protei.

Classic Porterhouse Steaks

Servings: 4
Cooking Time: 20 Minutes + Marinating Time
Ingredients:

- 1 ½ pounds Porterhouse steaks, cut into bite-sized chunks
- 1 teaspoon Montreal seasoning mix
- 2 tablespoons olive oil
- 2 garlic cloves, minced
- Sea salt and ground black pepper, to taste

Directions:

1. Add all the ingredients to a ceramic or glass bowl. Allow the beef to marinate for at least 3 hours.
2. Select the "Air Fry" function and adjust the temperature to 390 degrees F. Press the "Start" key. Place aluminum foil onto the drip pan.
3. When the display indicates "Add Food", place the beef in the air fryer oven perforated pan. Cook Porterhouse steaks for about 15 minutes.
4. Serve warm and enjoy!

Nutrition:

- Info418 Calories,29.3g Fat,0.9g Carbs,35.2g Protei.

Crispy Pork Tenderloin

Servings: 4
Cooking Time: 25 Minutes
Ingredients:

- 1 ½ pounds pork tenderloin
- 2 large eggs
- 1/2 cup all-purpose flour
- 1 teaspoon paprika
- Kosher salt and freshly ground black pepper, to taste
- 1 cup tortilla chips, crushed
- 2 tablespoons butter, melted

Directions:

1. Select the "Air Fry" function and adjust the temperature to 400 degrees F. Press the "Start" key. Now, brush the air fryer oven perforated pan with nonstick oil.
2. Mix the eggs, flour, and spices in a shallow bowl. In another shallow bowl, mix the tortilla chips and butter.
3. Coat the pork chops with the flour mixture; then, coat the pork chops with the tortilla chips mixture.
4. When the display indicates "Add Food", place the pork chops in the air fryer oven perforated pan.
5. Air fry them for 20 minutes or until the internal temperature reaches 145 degrees F on a meat thermometer.
6. Serve warm and enjoy!

Nutrition:

- Info455 Calories,23.2g Fat,18.6g Carbs,40.5g Protei.

Entrecôte Steak With Cauliflower

Servings: 4
Cooking Time: 20 Minutes
Ingredients:

- 1 ½ pounds Entrecôte steaks
- Salt and ground black pepper, to taste
- 1 tablespoon Dijon mustard
- 1 tablespoon olive oil
- 1 pound cauliflower florets

Directions:

1. Toss the steaks with salt, black pepper, mustard, and olive oil.

2. Select the "Air Fry" function and adjust the temperature to 380 degrees F. Press the "Start" key. Place aluminum foil onto the drip pan.

3. When the display indicates "Add Food", place the beef in the air fryer oven perforated pan. Reserve the marinade. Cook the beef for about 5 minutes.

4. Add in the cauliflower florets. Increase the temperature of the oven to 400 degrees F and continue to cook for 12 minutes more.

5. Serve warm and enjoy!

Nutrition:
- Info450 Calories,30.2g Fat,6.9g Carbs,37.6g Protei.

Sriracha Pork Burgers

Servings: 4
Cooking Time: 20 Minutes
Ingredients:
- 1 pound ground pork
- 1/2 cup instant oats
- 1 teaspoon dried basil
- 1 teaspoon dried oregano
- 1 medium onion, chopped
- 1 garlic clove, minced
- Sea salt and ground black pepper, to taste
- 4 hamburger buns
- 2 tablespoons sriracha

Directions:
1. Thoroughly combine the ground pork, instant oats, herbs, onion, garlic, salt, and black pepper.

2. Shape the mixture into four patties.

3. Select the "Air Fry" function and adjust the temperature to 370 degrees F. Press the "Start" key. Place aluminum foil onto the drip pan.

4. When the display indicates "Add Food", place the pork burgers in the air fryer oven perforated pan. Cook your burgers for about 8 minutes.

5. Flip the burgers over and continue to cook them for a further 8 minutes. Arrange your burgers with hamburger buns and sriracha sauce; add toppings of choice and enjoy!

Nutrition:
- Info430 Calories,29g Fat,27.3g Carbs,24.6g Protei.

Beef Brisket With Brussels Sprouts

Servings: 5
Cooking Time: 50 Minutes
Ingredients:
- 1 ½ pounds beef brisket
- 1 pound Brussels sprouts
- 2 garlic cloves, minced
- 1 teaspoon paprika
- Sea salt and ground black pepper, to taste
- 1/2 teaspoon ground cumin
- 1 teaspoon stone-ground mustard
- 2 tablespoons butter
- 1 cup barbecue sauce
- 1 tablespoon Worcestershire sauce

Directions:
1. Select the "Air Fry" function and adjust the temperature to 350 degrees F. Press the "Start" key.

2. Toss the beef and Brussels sprouts with the other ingredients. Place aluminum foil onto the drip pan.

3. When the display indicates "Add Food", place the beef in the air fryer oven perforated pan. Cook the beef for about 35 minutes.

4. Turn the temperature to 390 degrees F. Turn them over, add in the Brussels sprouts, and continue to cook for 15 minutes longer.

5. Serve warm and enjoy!

Nutrition:
- Info461 Calories,25.7g Fat,34g Carbs,24.2g Protei.

Blue Cheese-crusted Filet Mignon

Servings: 4
Cooking Time: 20 Minutes + Marinating Time
Ingredients:
- 1 ½ pounds fillet mignon
- 1 large egg, whisked
- 1 cup breadcrumbs
- 1 cup blue cheese, crumbled
- 2 tablespoons olive oil
- 1 garlic clove, minced
- 2 tablespoons fresh parsley, minced
- Coarse sea salt and ground black pepper, to taste

Directions:

1. Select the "Roast" function and adjust the temperature to 365 degrees F. Press the "Start" key.
2. Whisk the egg in a shallow bowl; in another shallow bowl, mix the remaining ingredients.
3. Dip the filet mignon into the whisked egg. Roll it into the cheese/crumb mixture.
4. When the display indicates "Add Food", place the beef in the air fryer oven perforated pan. Cook your fillet mignon for about 12 minutes.
5. Serve warm and enjoy!

Nutrition:

- Info473 Calories,28.1g Fat,7.8g Carbs,45.2g Protei.

Classic Beef Patties

Servings: 4

Cooking Time: 30 Minutes

Ingredients:

- 1 pound ground beef
- 1 carrot, grated
- 1 medium onion, chopped
- 1 teaspoon garlic, minced
- 2 tablespoons fresh cilantro, chopped
- 1 tablespoon fresh mint, chopped
- 1 tablespoon fresh parsley, chopped
- 1 tablespoon Worcestershire sauce
- A few drops of liquid smoke
- Sea salt and ground black pepper, to taste

Directions:

1. Select the "Air Fry" function and adjust the temperature to 390 degrees F. Press the "Start" key.
2. Place a sheet of parchment paper in the air fryer oven pan.
3. Mix all the ingredients until well combined.
4. Shape the mixture into four patties and place them in a single layer in the air fryer oven perforated pan.
5. Air fry the beef patties for 25 minutes. Bon appétit!

Nutrition:

- Info326 Calories,19.8g Fat,8.3g Carbs,30.3g Protei.

Parmesan Pork Blade Chops

Servings: 4

Cooking Time: 20 Minutes

Ingredients:

- 1 ½ pounds pork blade chops
- 1/2 cup all-purpose flour
- 1 teaspoon garlic powder
- 1 teaspoon onion powder
- 1/2 teaspoon dried oregano
- 1 teaspoon paprika
- 2 teaspoons olive oil
- 1/2 cup Parmesan cheese, grated

Directions:

1. Select the "Air Fry" function and adjust the temperature to 400 degrees F. Press the "Start" key. Now, grease the air fryer oven perforated pan with 1 teaspoon of olive oil.
2. Mix the flour and spices in a shallow bowl. In another shallow bowl, mix the remaining 1 teaspoon of olive oil and cheese.
3. Coat the pork chops with the flour mixture; then, coat the pork chops with the cheese mixture.
4. When the display indicates "Add Food", place the pork chops in the air fryer oven perforated pan.
5. Air fry them for 15 minutes or until the internal temperature reaches 145 degrees F on a meat thermometer.
6. Serve warm and enjoy!

Nutrition:

- Info379 Calories,15.9g Fat,15.1g Carbs,41.1g Protei.

Festive Round Roast

Servings: 6
Cooking Time: 50 Minutes
Ingredients:

- 2 ½ pounds round roast
- 1 teaspoon garlic, pressed
- 2 tablespoons olive oil
- 2 tablespoons Cajun seasoning blend

Directions:

1. Select the "Roast" function and adjust the temperature to 360 degrees F. Set the oven to "Rotate" and set the time to 45 minutes. Press the "Start" key.
2. Pat the beef dry. Rub the garlic, olive oil, and Cajun seasoning all over the round roast.
3. When the display indicates "Add Food", place the beef in the rotisserie basket.
4. Roast the beef until it reaches an internal temperature of 160 degrees F on a meat thermometer.
5. Bon appétit!

Nutrition:

- Info295 Calories,11.5g Fat,1.9g Carbs,42g Protei.

Asian-style Beef Bowl

Servings: 4
Cooking Time: 20 Minutes
Ingredients:

- 1 pound rib-eye steak, cubed
- 1/2 cup dashi (or beef bone stock)
- 4 tablespoons rice vinegar
- 2 tablespoons soy sauce (or Shoyu sauce)
- 1 teaspoon ginger-garlic paste
- 2 tablespoons agave nectar
- 1 teaspoon red pepper flakes, crushed
- Sea salt and ground black pepper, to taste
- 1 pound Chinese cabbage, cut into wedges
- 1 medium shallot, sliced

Directions:

1. Place the steak, dashi, rice vinegar, soy sauce, ginger-garlic paste, agave nectar, red pepper flakes, salt, and black pepper in a ceramic bowl. Cover and allow the beef to marinate for 3 hours.

2. Select the "Air Fry" function and adjust the temperature to 380 degrees F. Press the "Start" key. Place aluminum foil onto the drip pan.
3. When the display indicates "Add Food", place the steak, cabbage, and shallot in the parchment-lined air fryer oven perforated pan.
4. Cook the steak for about 8 minutes, turning it twice during the cooking time. Increase the temperature to 400 degrees F and continue cooking for 8 minutes more.
5. Serve warm and enjoy!

Nutrition:

- Info377 Calories,25.5g Fat,14.8g Carbs,23.3g Protei.

Festive Pork Butt

Servings: 5
Cooking Time: 35 Minutes + Marinating Time
Ingredients:

- 2 pounds boneless pork butt
- 2 tablespoons olive oil
- 2 tablespoons red wine vinegar
- 1 tablespoon Dijon mustard
- 1 teaspoon cumin seeds
- 1 teaspoon fennel seeds
- 1 teaspoon cayenne pepper
- Kosher salt and ground black pepper, to taste
- 2 tablespoons brown sugar

Directions:

1. Add all the ingredients to a ceramic or glass bowl. Allow the pork to marinate for at least 3 hours.
2. Select the "Air Fry" function and adjust the temperature to 390 degrees F. Press the "Start" key. Place aluminum foil onto the drip pan.
3. When the display indicates "Add Food", place the pork in the air fryer oven perforated pan. Reserve the marinade. Cook the pork for about 15 minutes.
4. Baste the pork with the reserved marinade and continue to roast for about 15 minutes or until cooked through. Serve immediately and enjoy!

Nutrition:

- Info542 Calories,37.5g Fat,3.1g Carbs,45.4g Protei.

Fish And Seafood Recipes

Easy Catfish Sandwiches

Servings: 4
Cooking Time: 15 Minutes
Ingredients:
- 1 pound catfish fillets
- 2 tablespoons fresh lemon juice
- 1 teaspoon paprika
- Sea salt and ground black pepper, to season
- 2 tablespoons olive oil
- 1 cup grape tomatoes, sliced
- 4 tablespoons fresh scallions, sliced
- 4 ciabatta rolls

Directions:
1. Select the "Air Fry" function and adjust the temperature to 400 degrees F. Set the oven to "Rotate" and set time to 10 minutes. Press the "Start" key.
2. In a mixing bowl, toss the fish with lemon juice, spices, and olive oil.
3. When the display indicates "Add Food", place the fish in the rotisserie basket.
4. Roast the fish until it is thoroughly cooked. Assemble your sandwiches with warm fish fillets, tomatoes, scallions, and ciabatta rolls.
5. Bon appétit!

Nutrition:
- Info353 Calories,12.6g Fat,33.8g Carbs,24.6g Protei.

Crab And Pea Patties

Servings: 4
Cooking Time: 15 Minutes
Ingredients:
- 3/4 pound lump crab meat
- 1 cup canned green peas, drained
- 1/2 cup seasoned breadcrumbs
- 1/4 cup celery, diced
- 4 tablespoons green onions, chopped
- 4 tablespoons mayonnaise

- 1 teaspoon brown mustard
- 2 tablespoons ketchup
- 4 tablespoons cheddar cheese, shredded
- 1 teaspoon smoked paprika
- 1 teaspoon dried oregano
- Kosher salt and ground black pepper, to taste

Directions:
1. Select the "Air Fry" function and adjust the temperature to 370 degrees F. Press the "Start" key.
2. Place a sheet of parchment paper in the air fryer oven pan.
3. Thoroughly combine all the ingredients in a mixing bowl. Form the mixture into patties and place them in a single layer in the air fryer oven perforated pan.
4. Air fry the patties for 10 minutes. Serve immediately and enjoy!

Nutrition:
- Info375 Calories,22.2g Fat,18.8g Carbs,21.2g Protei.

Favorite Halibut Steaks

Servings: 4
Cooking Time: 10 Minutes
Ingredients:
- 1 ½ pounds halibut steaks
- 2 tablespoons butter, melted
- 2 tablespoons lemon juice
- 1 tablespoon fresh basil, minced
- 1 tablespoon fresh mint, minced
- 1 tablespoon fresh parsley, minced
- 1/2 teaspoon garlic salt
- 1 teaspoon cayenne pepper
- 1/2 teaspoon ground black pepper

Directions:
1. Select the "Air Fry" function and adjust the temperature to 400 degrees F. Set the oven to "Rotate" and set time to 10 minutes. Press the "Start" key.

2.   In a mixing bowl, toss the fish with the other ingredients.

3.   When the display indicates "Add Food", place the fish in the rotisserie basket. Roast the fish until it flakes easily with a fork.

4.   Bon appétit!

Nutrition:

- Info253 Calories,14.4g Fat,7.9g Carbs,25.5g Protei.

Restaurant-style Fish Fingers

Servings: 5

Cooking Time: 15 Minutes

Ingredients:

- 1 ½ pounds cod fillets, cut into bite-sized strips
- 2 tablespoons olive oil
- 1 egg, beaten
- 1/4 cup milk
- 1 teaspoon garlic salt
- Freshly ground black pepper, to season
- 1/2 cup dry pancake mix
- 1/2 cup seasoned breadcrumbs

Directions:

1.   In a shallow bowl, mix the olive oil, egg, milk, garlic salt, black pepper, dry pancake mix.

2.   In another shallow bowl, mix the remaining ingredients.

3.   Dredge the fish strips in the oil/egg mixture. Then, dip the strips in the breadcrumb mixture, coating them completely and shaking off any excess.

4.   Select the "Air Fry" function and adjust the temperature to 400 degrees F. Press the "Start" key.

5.   Arrange the fish strips on the air fryer oven perforated pan, making sure not to crowd them. Air fry the fish for 10 minutes or until it is thoroughly cooked.

6.   Bon appétit!

Nutrition:

- Info255 Calories,7.4g Fat,18.6g Carbs,24.7g Protei.

Greek-style Fish Sticks

Servings: 4

Cooking Time: 15 Minutes

Ingredients:

- 1 pound codfish fillets, cut into strips
- 2 teaspoons olive oil
- 1 large egg
- 4 tablespoons Greek-style yogurt
- 1 teaspoon hot paprika
- 1 teaspoon Greek oregano
- Kosher salt and ground black pepper, to taste
- 1/2 cup all-purpose flour
- 1 cup seasoned breadcrumbs
- 1/4 cup parmesan cheese, grated

Directions:

1.   In a shallow bowl, mix the olive oil, egg, yogurt, spices. In another shallow bowl, mix the breadcrumbs and parmesan cheese, and flour.

2.   Dredge the fish strips in the egg/yogurt mixture. Then, dip the strips in the breadcrumb mixture, coating them completely and shaking off any excess.

3.   Select the "Air Fry" function and adjust the temperature to 400 degrees F. Press the "Start" key.

4.   Arrange the fish strips on the air fryer oven perforated pan, making sure not to crowd them. Air fry the fish for 10 minutes.

5.   Bon appétit!

Nutrition:

- Info325 Calories,6.4g Fat,34.8g Carbs,24.7g Protei.

Halibut Taco Wraps

Servings: 4

Cooking Time: 15 Minutes

Ingredients:

- 1 pound halibut fillets
- 2 teaspoon olive oil
- 1 teaspoon ancho chili powder
- 1/2 cup salsa, preferably homemade
- 1 ½ cups coleslaw mix
- 4 large corn tortillas (or flour tortillas)

Directions:

1. Select the "Air Fry" function and adjust the temperature to 400 degrees F. Set the oven to "Rotate" and set time to 10 minutes. Press the "Start" key.
2. Toss the fish with olive oil and chili powder; place the fish in the rotisserie basket. Air fry the fish for 10 minutes or until it is thoroughly cooked.
3. Cut the fish into strips.
4. Assemble your taco wraps with warm fish strips, salsa, coleslaw, and tortillas. Serve immediately and enjoy!

Nutrition:
- Info480 Calories,22.4g Fat,36.3g Carbs,22.6g Protei.

Old Bay Pollock Fillets

Servings: 4
Cooking Time: 15 Minutes
Ingredients:
- 1 pound pollock filets (or any other mild white fish)
- 1/2 cup all-purpose flour
- 1/2 cup breadcrumbs
- Kosher salt and cayenne pepper, to taste
- 1 teaspoon Old Bay seasoning mix
- 2 tablespoons butter, melted

Directions:
1. Select the "Air Fry" function and adjust the temperature to 400 degrees F. Set the time to 10 minutes. Press the "Start" key.
2. In a mixing bowl, toss the fish with the other ingredients.
3. When the display indicates "Add Food", place the fish in the parchment-lined air fryer oven perforated pan.
4. Air fry the fish until it flakes easily with a fork. Bon appétit!

Nutrition:
- Info235 Calories,7.2g Fat,16.2g Carbs,24.5g Protei.

Classic Fried Sea Scallops

Servings: 4
Cooking Time: 15 Minutes
Ingredients:

- 1 pound sea scallops
- 1 teaspoon garlic, minced
- 1 teaspoon onion powder
- 2 teaspoons olive oil
- Kosher salt and ground black pepper, to taste
- 1 teaspoon paprika
- 1 teaspoon dried basil
- 1 teaspoon dried oregano

Directions:
1. Select the "Air Fry" function and adjust the temperature to 400 degrees F. Press the "Start" key.
2. In a mixing bowl, toss the sea scallops with the other ingredients.
3. When the display indicates "Add Food", place the sea scallops in the air fryer oven perforated pan.
4. Air fry the sea scallops for 10 minutes or until pink and opaque.
5. Bon appétit!

Nutrition:
- Info346 Calories,6.8g Fat,4.6g Carbs,37.1g Protei.

Thai-style Shrimp

Servings: 4
Cooking Time: 10 Minutes
Ingredients:
- 1 pound shrimp, peeled and deveined
- 1/2 cup canned coconut milk
- 1/2 cup shredded coconut, unsweetened
- 1 teaspoon lime juice
- 2 garlic cloves, pressed
- 1 teaspoon hot paprika
- Kosher salt and ground black pepper, to taste
- 2 teaspoons olive oil

Directions:
1. Select the "Air Fry" function and adjust the temperature to 400 degrees F. Press the "Start" key.
2. In a mixing bowl, toss the shrimp with the remaining ingredients.
3. When the display indicates "Add Food", place the shrimp in the air fryer oven perforated pan.

4. Air fry the fish for 7 to 8 minutes or until pink and opaque. Enjoy!
5. Bon appétit!

Nutrition:
- Info135 Calories,4.6g Fat,5.8g Carbs,17g Protei.

Lemony Sea Bass Fillets

Servings: 4
Cooking Time: 15 Minutes
Ingredients:
- 1 pound sea bass fillets
- 1 lemon, squeezed
- 1/4 cup butter, softened
- 1 teaspoon cayenne pepper
- 1 teaspoon dried parsley flakes
- 1/2 teaspoon turmeric powder
- Kosher salt and ground black pepper, to season

Directions:
1. Select the "Air Fry" function and adjust the temperature to 400 degrees F. Set the oven to "Rotate" and set time to 10 minutes. Press the "Start" key.
2. In a mixing bowl, toss the fish with the other ingredients.
3. When the display indicates "Add Food", place the fish in the rotisserie basket.
4. Roast the fish until it is thoroughly cooked. Bon appétit!

Nutrition:
- Info225 Calories,13.9g Fat,2.4g Carbs,21.2g Protei.

Vegetable And Scallop Skewers

Servings: 4
Cooking Time: 10 Minutes
Ingredients:
- 1 pound sea scallops
- 1/2 pound cherry tomatoes
- 1/2 pound small mushrooms
- 1 tablespoon lemon juice
- 1 garlic clove, pressed
- 1 teaspoon Dijon mustard
- Coarse sea salt and ground black pepper, to taste
- 1 teaspoon cayenne pepper
- 1 teaspoon dried oregano

- 1 teaspoon dried rosemary
- 3 tablespoons butter

Directions:
1. Select the "Air Fry" function and adjust the temperature to 400 degrees F. Press the "Start" key.
2. Toss all the ingredients in a mixing bowl.
3. Thread bamboo skewers, alternating with scallops and veggies.
4. When the display indicates "Add Food", place the shrimp in the air fryer oven perforated pan. Air fry the skewers for 10 minutes or until pink and opaque.
5. Bon appétit!

Nutrition:
- Info188 Calories,9.7g Fat,9.8g Carbs,16.2g Protei.

Mini Smoked Salmon Frittatas

Servings: 4
Cooking Time: 15 Minutes
Ingredients:
- 12 ounces smoked salmon, chopped
- 6 eggs
- 1 ounce butter, softened
- 2 ounces cream cheese
- 1/4 cup sour cream
- 2 tablespoons fresh parsley, chopped
- 2 tablespoons fresh basil, chopped
- 2 tablespoons fresh scallions, chopped
- Sea salt and freshly ground black pepper, to season

Directions:
1. Select the "Bake" function and adjust the temperature to 350 degrees F and the time to 13 minutes. Press the "Start" key.
2. Meanwhile, brush silicone muffin cups with nonstick oil. Mix all the ingredients until well combined. Divide the mixture between the muffin cups.
3. When the display indicates "Add Food", place the muffin cups on the cooking tray in the center position.
4. Cook the mini fritters to your desired texture and serve warm. Bon appétit!

Nutrition:
- Info355 Calories,24.5g Fat,2.5g Carbs,27.3g Protei.

Herbed Salmon Steaks

Servings: 4
Cooking Time: 15 Minutes
Ingredients:
- 1 pound salmon steaks
- Kosher salt and freshly ground black pepper, to season
- 2 tablespoons olive oil
- 2 cloves garlic, pressed
- Fresh juice of 1 lemon
- 2 tablespoons agave nectar
- 2 tablespoons fresh parsley leaves, chopped
- 2 tablespoons fresh mint leaves, chopped

Directions:
1. Select the "Air Fry" function and adjust the temperature to 400 degrees F. Set the oven to "Rotate" and set time to 10 minutes. Press the "Start" key.
2. In a mixing bowl, toss the fish with the other ingredients.
3. When the display indicates "Add Food", place the fish in the rotisserie basket. Roast the fish until it flakes easily with a fork.
4. Bon appétit!

Nutrition:
- Info346 Calories,6.8g Fat,4.6g Carbs,37.1g Protei.

Hot Sardine Cutlets

Servings: 4
Cooking Time: 15 Minutes
Ingredients:
- 10 ounces sardines, drained and chopped
- 1 large egg, well-beaten
- 1 tablespoon ground chia seeds
- 1 medium onion, chopped
- 2 garlic cloves, minced
- 1 carrot, grated
- 2 tablespoons butter, softened
- 2 tablespoons mayonnaise

- 1 teaspoon Sriracha sauce
- Kosher salt and ground black pepper, to season
- 1 teaspoon smoked paprika
- 1/2 cup seasoned breadcrumbs

Directions:
1. Select the "Air Fry" function and adjust the temperature to 390 degrees F. Press the "Start" key.
2. Place a sheet of parchment paper in the air fryer oven pan. Thoroughly combine all the ingredients.
3. Form the mixture into equal patties and place them in a single layer in the air fryer oven perforated pan.
4. Air fry the patties for 13 minutes, turning them over halfway through.
5. Bon appétit!

Nutrition:
- Info320 Calories,17.6g Fat,16.3g Carbs,20.3g Protei.

Creole Catfish Fillets

Servings: 4
Cooking Time: 15 Minutes
Ingredients:
- 1 pound catfish fillets
- 2 eggs, beaten
- 1/2 cup all-purpose flour
- 1/2 cup breadcrumbs
- 1 teaspoon Creole seasoning mix
- 2 teaspoons olive oil
- 1 tablespoon fresh parsley, chopped
- 1 tablespoon fresh cilantro, chopped

Directions:
1. Select the "Air Fry" function and adjust the temperature to 400 degrees F. Set the time to 10 minutes. Press the "Start" key.
2. Pat the fish dry. In a shallow bowl, whisk the eggs with the flour. In a shallow bowl, mix the remaining ingredients.
3. Dip the fish into the egg mixture. Then, roll the fish over the breadcrumb mixture.
4. When the display indicates "Add Food", place the fish in the parchment-lined air fryer oven perforated pan.
5. Air fry the fish until it flakes easily with a fork. Bon appétit!

Paprika Shrimp Salad

Servings: 4
Cooking Time: 10 Minutes + Chilling Time
Ingredients:
- 1 pound shrimp, peeled and chilled
- 2 stalks celery, diced
- 1 red onion, chopped
- 2 garlic cloves, minced
- 2 hard-boiled eggs, peeled and diced
- 1 small cucumber, sliced
- 1 tablespoon fresh dill, minced
- 1/2 cup mayonnaise
- 1 tablespoon Dijon mustard
- 1 teaspoon paprika
- Kosher salt and ground black pepper, to taste

Directions:
1. Select the "Air Fry" function and adjust the temperature to 400 degrees F. Press the "Start" key.
2. In a mixing bowl, toss the shrimp with the remaining ingredients.
3. When the display indicates "Add Food", place the shrimp in the air fryer oven perforated pan. Air fry the shrimp for 7 to 8 minutes or until pink and opaque.
4. Toss your shrimp with the other salad ingredients and serve well-chilled.
5. Bon appétit!

Nutrition:
- Info352 Calories,24.4g Fat,5.2g Carbs,27g Protei.

Street-style Fish Fritters

Servings: 5
Cooking Time: 15 Minutes
Ingredients:
- 1 ½ pounds haddock, chopped (or any other mild white fish)
- 2 ounces bacon bits

- 1 zucchini, grated
- 1 medium onion, diced
- 2 garlic cloves, minced
- 1 chili pepper, chopped
- 2 medium eggs, beaten
- ¼ cup full-fat milk
- 1 cup instant oats
- 1 teaspoon baking powder

Directions:
1. Select the "Air Fry" function and adjust the temperature to 390 degrees F. Press the "Start" key.
2. Place a sheet of parchment paper in the air fryer oven pan. Thoroughly combine all the ingredients.
3. Form the mixture into four patties and place them in a single layer in the air fryer oven perforated pan.
4. Air fry the patties for 12 minutes, turning them over halfway through. Serve warm and enjoy!

Nutrition:
- Info315 Calories,9.4g Fat,24.8g Carbs,32.2g Protei.

Father's Day Fish Tacos

Servings: 4
Cooking Time: 15 Minutes
Ingredients:
- 1 pound tilapia fillets (or other mild white fish)
- 1 tablespoon butter, melted
- 1 teaspoon red pepper flakes
- 1/2 teaspoon cumin
- 1 teaspoon paprika
- Sea salt and ground black pepper, to taste
- 1 teaspoon Mexican oregano
- 1 teaspoon garlic, minced
- Tacos:
- 4 medium flour tortillas
- 1 avocado, pitted and sliced
- 1 tomato, thinly sliced
- 1 red onion, thinly sliced

Directions:

1. Select the "Air Fry" function and adjust the temperature to 400 degrees F. Set the oven to "Rotate" and set time to 10 minutes. Press the "Start" key.
2. In a mixing bowl, toss the fish with the melted butter, spices, and garlic.
3. When the display indicates "Add Food", place the fish in the rotisserie basket.
4. Roast the fish until it is thoroughly cooked. Cut your fish into strips; assemble your tacos with the fish and other ingredients.
5. Bon appétit!

Nutrition:
- Info363 Calories,15.1g Fat,29.6g Carbs,28.5g Protei.

Ultimate Tuna Melts

Servings: 4
Cooking Time: 15 Minutes
Ingredients:
- 12 ounces canned albacore tuna, drained
- 4 Hawaiian sweet rolls, split
- 1/2 cup mayonnaise
- 4 slices cheddar cheese
- 2 tablespoons scallions, chopped

Directions:
1. Select the "Broil" function and adjust the temperature to 400 degrees F. Set the time to 12 minutes. Press the "Start" key.
2. Assemble the sandwiches by laying out the rolls and, then, adding the remaining ingredients. Spritz the sandwiches with nonstick oil.
3. When the display indicates "Add Food", place the sandwiches in the parchment-lined air fryer oven perforated pan.
4. Bake your sandwiches for 6 minutes, flip them over, spritz with nonstick oil and continue baking for 6 minutes more.
5. Serve immediately.

Nutrition:
- Info445 Calories,32.2g Fat,15.1g Carbs,2.6g Protei.

Favorite Seafood Fritters

Servings: 4
Cooking Time: 15 Minutes
Ingredients:
- 1 pound shrimp, peeled and deveined
- 1 large sweet onion, chopped
- 1 teaspoon garlic, pressed
- 1 bell pepper, chopped
- 1/2 cup all-purpose flour
- 1/2 cup tortilla chips, crushed
- 2 teaspoons butter, melted
- 1 teaspoon baking powder
- 1 teaspoon Cajun seasoning mix
- Sea salt and freshly ground black pepper, to taste
- 1 teaspoon paprika
- 1 teaspoon stone-ground mustard
- 2 large eggs, beaten
- 1⁄4 cup cream of celery soup

Directions:
1. Select the "Air Fry" function and adjust the temperature to 370 degrees F. Press the "Start" key.
2. Place a sheet of parchment paper in the air fryer oven pan.
3. Thoroughly combine all the ingredients in a mixing bowl. Form the mixture into equal patties and place them in a single layer in the air fryer oven perforated pan.
4. Air fry the fritters for 13 minutes. Serve warm and enjoy!

Nutrition:
- Info345 Calories,10.4g Fat,32.8g Carbs,30.1g Protei.

Rice, Grains And Pastry Recipes

Greek-style Quinoa Croquettes

Servings: 4
Cooking Time: 20 Minutes
Ingredients:

- 2 cups quinoa, cooked and rinsed
- 1 large egg
- 2 tablespoons tapioca flour
- 3 tablespoons instant oats
- 1 medium carrot, finely chopped
- 1 medium onion, finely chopped
- 1 bell pepper, chopped
- 2 cloves garlic, pressed
- 2 tablespoons fresh parsley, chopped
- Sea salt and ground black pepper, to taste
- 1 cup feta cheese, crumbled

Directions:

1. Select the "Air Fry" function and adjust the temperature to 400 degrees F. Press the "Start" key.
2. Place a sheet of parchment paper in the air fryer oven pan. Thoroughly combine all the ingredients.
3. Form the mixture into equal balls and place them in a single layer in the air fryer oven perforated pan.
4. Air fry the croquettes for 15 minutes or until golden brown. Serve hot and enjoy!

Nutrition:

- Info285 Calories,11.4g Fat,35.2g Carbs,12.7g Protei.

Chinese-style Rice Balls

Servings: 4
Cooking Time: 15 Minutes
Ingredients:

- 2 cups whole-wheat rice, cooked
- 1/2 cup rice flour
- 1/2 pound beef sausage, crumbled
- 2 tablespoons rice wine
- 2 tablespoons soy sauce
- 1 teaspoon agave syrup
- 2 green onion stalks, minced
- 1 teaspoon ginger-garlic paste
- 2 tablespoons fresh parsley, minced
- Sea salt and ground black pepper, to season
- 1 cup breadcrumbs
- 2 large eggs, beaten
- 2 teaspoons sesame oil

Directions:

1. Select the "Air Fry" function and adjust the temperature to 400 degrees F. Press the "Start" key.
2. Place a sheet of parchment paper in the air fryer oven pan. Thoroughly combine all the ingredients.
3. Form the mixture into equal balls and place them in a single layer in the air fryer oven perforated pan.
4. Air fry the croquettes for 11 minutes or until golden brown. Serve hot and enjoy!

Nutrition:

- Info473 Calories,22.7g Fat,50.1g Carbs,15.6g Protei.

Italian-style Oatmeal Cheeseburgers

Servings: 4
Cooking Time: 20 Minutes
Ingredients:

- 2 cups quick-cooking oats
- 1 small onion, chopped
- 2 tablespoons olive oil
- 1/2 cup cheddar cheese, shredded
- 2 garlic cloves, minced
- 1 tablespoon Italian seasoning mix
- 1 teaspoon smoked paprika
- Sea salt and ground black pepper, to taste

Directions:

1. Select the "Air Fry" function and adjust the temperature to 400 degrees F. Press the "Start" key.
2. Place a sheet of parchment paper in the air fryer oven pan. Thoroughly combine all the ingredients.

3. Form the mixture into equal patties and place them in a single layer in the air fryer oven perforated pan.

4. Air fry the patties for 15 minutes or until golden brown. Serve hot and enjoy!

Nutrition:

- Info385 Calories,12.4g Fat,56.3g Carbs,13.7g Protei.

Quiche Pastry Cups

Servings: 6

Cooking Time: 15 Minutes

Ingredients:

- 1 can refrigerated crescent rolls
- 2 large eggs
- 1 cup pasta sauce
- 4 ounces cup Gruyere cheese, shredded

Directions:

1. Spritz 6 standard-size muffin cups with nonstick spray.

2. Cut your dough evenly into 6 squares. Press your dough pieces into muffin cups.

3. Thoroughly combine the eggs, pasta sauce, and cheese; divide the mixture between the muffin cups.

4. Bake the pastry cups at 350 degrees F for about 7 minutes. Serve warm and enjoy!

Nutrition:

- Info227 Calories,10.1g Fat,22.9g Carbs,11.1g Protei.

Spelt Burgers With Herbs

Servings: 4

Cooking Time: 20 Minutes

Ingredients:

- 2 cups hulled spelt, cooked
- 1 carrot, grated
- 2 tablespoons parsley, chopped
- 2 tablespoons cilantro, chopped
- 2 tablespoons scallions, chopped
- 1/2 cup goat cheese, grated
- 1 egg
- Sea salt and freshly ground pepper, to taste

Directions:

1. Select the "Air Fry" function and adjust the temperature to 400 degrees F. Press the "Start" key.

2. Place a sheet of parchment paper in the air fryer oven pan. Thoroughly combine all the ingredients.

3. Form the mixture into equal patties and place them in a single layer in the air fryer oven perforated pan.

4. Air fry the patties for 15 minutes or until golden brown. Serve hot and enjoy!

Nutrition:

- Info365 Calories,7.4g Fat,63g Carbs,17.8g Protei.

Japanese-style Yaki Onigiri

Servings: 4

Cooking Time: 15 Minutes

Ingredients:

- 2 cups Japanese sushi rice, cooked and rinsed
- 2 tablespoons Shoyu sauce
- 2 tablespoons sesame seeds
- 2 teaspoons sesame oil
- Sea salt and crushed red pepper flakes, to taste

Directions:

1. Select the "Air Fry" function and adjust the temperature to 400 degrees F. Press the "Start" key.

2. Place a sheet of parchment paper in the air fryer oven pan. Thoroughly combine all the ingredients.

3. Form the mixture into equal balls and place them in a single layer in the air fryer oven perforated pan.

4. Air fry the croquettes for 11 minutes or until golden brown. Serve hot and enjoy!

Nutrition:

- Info195 Calories,6.8g Fat,27.2g Carbs,6.2g Protei.

Wild Rice Patties

Servings: 4
Cooking Time: 15 Minutes
Ingredients:

- 2 cups cooked wild rice
- 1 cup plain flour
- 2 eggs, well-beaten
- 1 shallot, chopped
- 2 garlic cloves, minced
- Sea salt and ground black pepper, to taste
- 2 tablespoons olive oil

Directions:

1. Select the "Air Fry" function and adjust the temperature to 400 degrees F. Press the "Start" key.
2. Place a sheet of parchment paper in the air fryer oven pan. Thoroughly combine all the ingredients.
3. Form the mixture into equal patties and place them in a single layer in the air fryer oven perforated pan.
4. Air fry the patties for 11 minutes or until golden brown. Serve hot and enjoy!

Nutrition:

- Info295 Calories,9.4g Fat,43.3g Carbs,9.7g Protei.

Homemade Pita Chips

Servings: 2
Cooking Time: 10 Minutes
Ingredients:

- 2 small pita bread pockets, cut into triangles
- 2 tablespoons extra-virgin olive oil
- Coarse sea salt and ground black pepper, to taste
- 1 teaspoon dried oregano

Directions:

1. Select the "Air Fry" function and adjust the temperature to 330 degrees F. Press the "Start" key.
2. Toss the pita triangles with olive oil and salt.
3. Bake your pita chips for 6 minutes or until lightly browned; toss the pita chips once or twice, working in batches.
4. Bon appétit!

Nutrition:

- Info207 Calories,13.9g Fat,18.2g Carbs,3.1g Protei.

Buffalo-style Pizza

Servings: 1
Cooking Time: 15 Minutes
Ingredients:

- 1 pizza dough
- 1 teaspoon olive oil
- 4 tablespoons pasta sauce
- 2 ounces smoked chicken sausage, sliced
- 2 teaspoons parmesan cheese, grated

Directions:

1. Select the "Air Fry" function and adjust the temperature to 400 degrees F. Press the "Start" key.
2. Stretch the dough on a work surface. Spread the dough with olive oil and pasta sauce.
3. Top with sausage and cheese. Place your pizza on the air fryer tray that is previously greased with olive oil.
4. Bake your pizza for 10 minutes. Serve warm and enjoy!

Nutrition:

- Info379 Calories,14.9g Fat,44.9g Carbs,16.6g Protei.

Spicy Oatmeal Patties

Servings: 4
Cooking Time: 20 Minutes
Ingredients:

- 1 ½ cups rolled oats
- 1/2 cup plain flour
- 2 tablespoons olive oil, divided
- 1 medium onion, chopped
- 2 garlic cloves, minced
- 2 eggs, beaten
- 1 teaspoon red pepper flakes, crushed
- 1 teaspoon ground coriander
- 2 tablespoons parsley, chopped
- 2 tablespoons cilantro, chopped
- 2 tablespoons chives, chopped
- 1 cup Cheddar cheese, shredded

- Sea salt and ground black pepper, to taste

Directions:

1. Select the "Air Fry" function and adjust the temperature to 400 degrees F. Press the "Start" key.

2. Place a sheet of parchment paper in the air fryer oven pan. Thoroughly combine all the ingredients.

3. Form the mixture into equal patties and place them in a single layer in the air fryer oven perforated pan.

4. Air fry the patties for 15 minutes or until golden brown. Serve hot and enjoy!

Nutrition:
- Info500 Calories,22.4g Fat,55.3g Carbs,21.7g Protei.

Corn Bacon Waffles

Servings: 4
Cooking Time: 20 Minutes

Ingredients:
- 2 ounces smoked bacon bits
- 1 cup plain flour
- 1 cup cornflour
- 1/2 stick butter, at room temperature
- 1 teaspoons baking powder
- 1/2 teaspoon baking soda
- 1/4 teaspoon salt
- 1 cup buttermilk
- 1 large egg, whisked

Directions:

1. In a mixing bowl, thoroughly combine the dry ingredients. In another bowl, whisk the wet ingredients. Add the wet mixture to the dry ingredients, and mix to combine well.

2. Grease a baking pan with nonstick cooking oil and set it aside. Spoon the batter onto the pan and place the pan onto the air fryer tray.

3. Select the "Air Fry" function and adjust the temperature to 350 degrees F. Press the "Start" key.

4. Air fry the waffles for about 15 minutes, working in batches, if needed. Enjoy!

Nutrition:

- Info425 Calories,20.4g Fat,49.3g Carbs,10.8g Protei.

Mushroom And Oatmeal Fritters

Servings: 4
Cooking Time: 20 Minutes

Ingredients:
- 2 cups instant oats
- 1 cup cremini mushrooms, chopped
- 1 medium onion, finely chopped
- 2 garlic cloves, minced
- 2 tablespoons butter, room temperature
- 2 tablespoons marinara sauce
- 2 eggs, whisked

Directions:

1. Select the "Air Fry" function and adjust the temperature to 400 degrees F. Press the "Start" key.

2. Place a sheet of parchment paper in the air fryer oven pan. Thoroughly combine all the ingredients.

3. Form the mixture into equal patties and place them in a single layer in the air fryer oven perforated pan.

4. Air fry your fritters for 15 minutes or until golden brown.

5. Bon appétit!

Nutrition:
- Info407 Calories,13.3g Fat,56.3g Carbs,17.2g Protei.

Easy Pepperoni Pizza

Servings: 1
Cooking Time: 15 Minutes
Ingredients:
- 1 pizza crust
- 1/4 cup pizza sauce
- 1 ounce pepperoni, sliced
- 1 small bell pepper, seeded and sliced
- 1 ounce mozzarella cheese, crumbled

Directions:
1. Select the "Air Fry" function and adjust the temperature to 400 degrees F. Press the "Start" key.
2. Stretch the dough on a work surface lightly dusted with flour. Spread with a layer of pizza sauce.
3. Top with pepperoni, bell pepper, and cheese. Place your pizza on the air fryer tray that is previously greased with olive oil.
4. Bake your pizza for 10 minutes. Serve warm and enjoy!

Nutrition:
- Info423 Calories,17.3g Fat,43.2g Carbs,22.1g Protei.

Italian-style Mini Pies

Servings: 4
Cooking Time: 15 Minutes
Ingredients:
- 1 can refrigerated crescent dough
- 1 medium carrot, grated
- 8 ounces button mushrooms, chopped
- 1 teaspoon Italian seasoning mix
- 1 cup marinara sauce

Directions:
1. Spritz 6 standard-size muffin cups with nonstick spray.
2. Cut your dough evenly into 6 squares. Press your dough pieces into muffin cups.
3. Thoroughly combine the carrot, mushroom, seasonings, and marinara sauce; divide the mixture between the muffin cups.
4. Bake your pastry cups at 350 degrees F for about 7 minutes. Serve warm and enjoy!

Nutrition:
- Info209 Calories,3.8g Fat,37.9g Carbs,6.9g Protei.

Toasted Greek Pita

Servings: 2
Cooking Time: 10 Minutes
Ingredients:
- 2 large whole-wheat pitas
- 1/2 cup hummus
- 1 small onion, chopped
- 2 ounces feta cheese, crumbled
- 1 small tomato, sliced
- 2 tablespoons Kalamata olives, pitted and sliced
- Sea salt and ground black pepper, to season

Directions:
1. Assemble pita breads with the other ingredients; you can use a toothpick to secure your pitas.
2. Select the "Toast" function and press the "Start" key.
3. When the display indicates "Add Food", place the sandwich on the air fryer tray.
4. Toast the sandwich for about 3 minutes or so. Enjoy!

Nutrition:
- Info379 Calories,14g Fat,52.9g Carbs,13.8g Protei.

Classic Tortilla Chips

Servings: 4
Cooking Time: 5 Minutes
Ingredients:
- 4 corn tortillas, cut into triangles
- 1 tablespoon olive oil
- Sea salt, to taste

Directions:
1. Select the "Air Fry" function and adjust the temperature to 390 degrees F. Press the "Start" key.
2. Toss your tortilla pieces with olive oil and salt.
3. Bake your chips for 3 minutes or until lightly browned; cook in batches.
4. Bon appétit!

Easy Cinnamon Donuts

Servings: 8
Cooking Time: 15 Minutes
Ingredients:

- 1 can jumbo biscuits
- 4 teaspoons butter melted
- 1/2 cup granulated sugar
- 1 teaspoon ground cinnamon

Directions:

1. Select the "Air Fry" function and adjust the temperature to 375 degrees F. Press the "Start" key.
2. Spritz the air fryer oven perforated pan with cooking oil. Separate the dough into eight biscuits.
3. Bake in the preheated air fryer for 4 minutes. Flip the donuts and air fry for an additional 4 minutes.
4. Mix the butter, sugar, and cinnamon. Then, cover the donuts with the sugar mixture by dipping and rolling around.
5. Bon appétit!

Nutrition:

- Info156 Calories,4.9g Fat,25.8g Carbs,1.9g Protei.

Easy Breakfast Granola

Servings: 10
Cooking Time: 45 Minutes
Ingredients:

- 1 ½ cups rolled oats
- 1 cup walnuts
- 1/2 cup pine nuts
- 1/2 cup pumpkin seeds, hulled
- 1/2 cup sunflower seeds, hulled
- 1/4 cup maple syrup
- 2 tablespoons coconut oil
- 1 teaspoon cinnamon
- 1/2 teaspoon ground cinnamon
- A pinch of sea salt

- A pinch of grated nutmeg
- 1/2 cup flaked coconut

Directions:

1. Select the "Air Fry" function and adjust the temperature to 260 degrees F. Press the "Start" key.
2. Line the air fryer tray with a piece of parchment paper.
3. Thoroughly combine all ingredients and spread the mixture onto the parchment-lined air fryer tray.
4. Bake your granola for 40 minutes, rotating the pan once or twice during cooking.
5. This granola can be kept in an airtight container for up to 2 weeks. Bon appétit!

Nutrition:

- Info323 Calories,22g Fat,26g Carbs,9.7g Protei.

Mediterranean-style Calzone

Servings: 2
Cooking Time: 15 Minutes
Ingredients:

- 2 large lavash flatbread
- 2 teaspoon olive oil
- 1/4 cup marinara sauce
- 4 ounces parmesan cheese, grated
- 2 ounces black olives, pitted and sliced
- 1 teaspoon dried oregano
- 1 teaspoon dried basil

Directions:

1. Select the "Air Fry" function and adjust the temperature to 390 degrees F. Press the "Start" key.
2. Assemble the Mediterranean calzone with lavash and the remaining ingredients. Fold the lavash bread in half, and pat the edges so that it is tightly closed.
3. Bake your Mediterranean calzone for 8 minutes or until lightly browned.
4. Bon appétit!

Nutrition:

- Info518 Calories,30.6g Fat,35.5g Carbs,23.6g Protei.

Mexican-style Bulgur Patties

Servings: 4
Cooking Time: 20 Minutes
Ingredients:

- 2 cups bulgur wheat
- 2 tablespoons olive oil
- 1 tablespoon tomato paste
- 1 teaspoon Mexican oregano
- 1 teaspoon ancho chili powder
- 1 teaspoon cayenne pepper
- Kosher salt and ground black pepper, to taste
- 1 teaspoon lime zest
- 1 medium onion, chopped
- 2 garlic cloves, minced
- 1 cup canned or boiled pinto beans, rinsed
- 1/2 cup Mexican-blend cheese, shredded
- 1/2 cup tortilla chips, crushed

Directions:
1. Select the "Air Fry" function and adjust the temperature to 400 degrees F. Press the "Start" key.
2. Place a sheet of parchment paper in the air fryer oven pan. Thoroughly combine all the ingredients.
3. Form the mixture into equal patties and place them in a single layer in the air fryer oven perforated pan.
4. Air fry the patties for 15 minutes or until cooked through. Serve hot and enjoy!

Nutrition:
- Info353 Calories,15.1g Fat,45g Carbs,11.9g Protei.

Poultry Recipes

Kid-friendly Chicken Nuggets

Servings: 5
Cooking Time: 20 Minutes
Ingredients:

- 1 teaspoon olive oil
- 2 pounds boneless, skinless chicken breasts, cut into 1-inch-thick strips
- 1 egg, beaten
- 1 cup all-purpose flour
- Coarse sea salt and ground black pepper, to taste
- 1 cup tortilla chips, crushed

Directions:
1. Select the "Air Fry" function and adjust the temperature to 350 degrees F. Press the "Start" key. Then, grease the air fryer oven perforated pan with olive oil.
2. Pat the chicken dry and set it aside.
3. In a shallow bowl, whisk the egg until pale and frothy; gradually add in the flour, salt, and black pepper. Add the chicken tenders to the bowl and toss until well coated on all sides.
4. In another shallow bowl, place the crushed tortilla chips. Roll the chicken strips over the crushed tortilla chips until well coated on all sides.
5. When the display indicates "Add Food", place the tenders in the air fryer oven perforated pan. Air fry them for 15 minutes.
6. Serve warm and enjoy!

Nutrition:
- Info440 Calories,13.2g Fat,37.5g Carbs,42.4g Protei.

Juicy Turkey Breasts

Servings: 5
Cooking Time: 45 Minutes
Ingredients:
- 2 pounds turkey breasts, boneless and skinless
- 1 cup buttermilk
- 2 garlic cloves, minced
- 2 tablespoons olive oil
- 1 tablespoon Dijon mustard
- 1 sprig fresh rosemary, chopped
- 1 sprig fresh thyme, chopped
- Kosher salt and freshly ground black pepper, to taste

Directions:
1. Place all the ingredients in a ceramic dish; let it marinate for about 1 hour.
2. Select the "Roast" function and adjust the temperature to 370 degrees F. Press the "Start" key.
3. Place the turkey in the air fryer oven perforated pan. Place aluminum foil onto the drip pan.
4. Roast the turkey for about 20 minutes; flip it over and cook for 15 minutes longer or until the turkey reaches an internal temperature of 170 degrees F on a meat thermometer.
5. Let the turkey rest for 10 minutes before slicing and serving. Enjoy!

Nutrition:
- Info386 Calories,18.6g Fat,2.8g Carbs,42.2g Protei.

Grandma's Chicken Roulade

Servings: 4
Cooking Time: 25 Minutes
Ingredients:
- 1 pound chicken fillets
- Sea salt and ground black pepper, to taste
- 1 cup goat cheese, crumbled
- 1 teaspoon fresh thyme leaves, chopped
- 1 teaspoon fresh rosemary leaves, chopped
- 4 ounces smoked bacon, diced
- 1 bell pepper, seeded and diced

Directions:

1. Select the "Air Fry" function and adjust the temperature to 360 degrees F. Press the "Start" key.
2. Place a sheet of parchment paper in the air fryer oven pan.
3. Pat the chicken dry and season them with salt and black pepper.
4. In a mixing bowl, thoroughly combine the remaining ingredients. Divide the stuffing between the chicken fillets and roll them up.
5. Arrange the chicken rolls in the air fryer oven perforated pan.
6. Air fry the chicken rolls for about 10 minutes; flip it over and cook for 10 minutes longer or until the chicken reaches an internal temperature of 160 degrees F on a meat thermometer.
7. Bon appétit!

Nutrition:
- Info492 Calories,38.2g Fat,2.7g Carbs,33.2g Protei.

Louisiana-style Stuffed Chicken

Servings: 4
Cooking Time: 25 Minutes
Ingredients:
- 1 ½ pound chicken fillets
- Sea salt and ground black pepper, to taste
- 1 teaspoon cayenne pepper
- 2 tablespoons Louisiana-style hot sauce
- 8 ounces smoked pork sausage, crumbled
- 6 ounces parmesan cheese, grated
- 1 cup breadcrumbs

Directions:
1. Select the "Air Fry" function and adjust the temperature to 360 degrees F. Press the "Start" key.
2. Pat the chicken dry and season them with salt, black pepper, and cayenne pepper.
3. In a mixing bowl, thoroughly combine the hot sauce, sausage, and cheese. Divide the stuffing between the chicken fillets and roll them up.
4. Roll them over the breadcrumbs and secure with toothpicks.
5. Air fry the stuffed chicken for about 10 minutes; flip it over and cook for 10 minutes longer or until the chicken

reaches an internal temperature of 160 degrees F on a meat thermometer.

6. Bon appétit!

Nutrition:

- Info602 Calories,34.6g Fat,13.3g Carbs,56.1g Protei.

Classic Turkey Burgers

Servings: 4
Cooking Time: 20 Minutes
Ingredients:

- 1 tablespoon olive oil
- 1 pound ground chicken
- 1/2 cup crackers, crushed
- 1 small onion, chopped
- 2 cloves garlic, minced
- 1 egg, beaten
- Sea salt and ground black pepper, to taste

Directions:

1. Select the "Air Fry" function and adjust the temperature to 340 degrees F. Press the "Start" key.
2. Place a sheet of parchment paper in the air fryer oven pan.
3. Mix all the ingredients until well combined. Shape the mixture into four patties and place them in a single layer in the air fryer oven perforated pan.
4. Air fry the turkey burgers for 15 minutes or until they reach an internal temperature of 165 degrees F.
5. Bon appétit!

Nutrition:

- Info322 Calories,23.2g Fat,3.6g Carbs,23.8g Protei.

Paprika Roast Turkey

Servings: 5
Cooking Time: 20 Minutes
Ingredients:

- 2 pounds turkey, giblet removed, rinsed, and pat dry
- 2 tablespoons olive oil
- 1 teaspoon smoked paprika

- Coarse sea salt and freshly ground black pepper, to season
- 1 teaspoon fresh rosemary, chopped
- 2 tablespoons fresh green onion, chopped
- 4 garlic cloves, chopped
- 2 bell peppers, chopped

Directions:

1. Stuff the turkey with the other ingredients. Using the rotisserie spit, push through the turkey and attach the rotisserie forks.
2. Select the "Roast" function and adjust the temperature to 350 degrees F. Set the oven to "Rotate" and set time to 3 hours. Press the "Start" key.
3. When the display indicates "Add Food", place the prepared turkey in the oven.
4. Roast the turkey until the internal temperature reaches 170 degrees F on a meat thermometer.
5. Let the turkey rest for 10 minutes before carving and serving. Enjoy!

Nutrition:

- Info425 Calories,34.4g Fat,2.1g Carbs,24.6g Protei.

Kid-friendly Chicken Croquettes

Servings: 4
Cooking Time: 20 Minutes
Ingredients:

- 2 tablespoons unsalted butter
- 1 pound ground chicken
- 2 ounces, bacon
- Sea salt and freshly ground pepper, to taste
- 1 cup breadcrumbs
- 1/4 cup whole milk
- 2 medium eggs

Directions:

1. Select the "Air Fry" function and adjust the temperature to 350 degrees F. Press the "Start" key.
2. Place a sheet of parchment paper in the air fryer oven pan.
3. In a mixing bowl, thoroughly combine all the ingredients. Then, drop rounds of the mixture in a single layer onto the prepared pan using a small scoop.

4. Air fry the croquettes for 10 minutes; turn the croquettes over and increase the temperature to 400 degrees F. Air fry for a further 5 minutes to brown the outsides of the croquettes.

5. Bon appétit!

Nutrition:
- Info397 Calories,28.1g Fat,8.5g Carbs,27.1g Protei.

Blue Cheese Chicken Drumettes

Servings: 4
Cooking Time: 25 Minutes
Ingredients:
- 1 ½ pounds chicken drumettes
- 5 tablespoons butter, melted
- 1 cup blue cheese, crumbled, divided
- 1/2 cup heavy cream
- 1 teaspoon Worcestershire sauce

Directions:
1. Select the "Air Fry" function and adjust the temperature to 375 degrees F. Press the "Start" key.
2. Place a sheet of parchment paper in the air fryer oven pan. Toss the chicken drumettes with butter.
3. To make the sauce, whisk the cheese, heavy cream, and Worcestershire sauce until well combined.
4. Arrange the chicken drumettes in a single layer in the air fryer oven perforated pan.
5. Air fry the chicken drumettes for 10 minutes. Spoon the sauce over them and air fry them for 10 minutes more.
6. Bon appétit!

Nutrition:
- Info484 Calories,34.2g Fat,1.4g Carbs,42.2g Protei.

Herbed Chicken Drumsticks

Servings: 4
Cooking Time: 30 Minutes
Ingredients:
- 1 ½ pounds chicken drumsticks
- 2 teaspoons olive
- 1 teaspoon paprika
- Kosher salt and ground black pepper, to taste

- 1 teaspoon garlic powder
- 2 sprigs rosemary, chopped
- 1 sprig thyme, chopped

Directions:
1. Select the "Air Fry" function and adjust the temperature to 400 degrees F. Press the "Start" key.
2. Lightly grease the air fryer oven perforated pan with olive oil.
3. Poke about 10 holes in the skin of each drumstick. Toss the chicken drumsticks with the remaining ingredients.
4. When the display indicates "Add Food", place the drumsticks in the air fryer oven perforated pan.
5. Roast the chicken drumsticks for about 25 minutes, flipping them halfway through cooking.
6. Bon appétit!

Nutrition:
- Info378 Calories,21.8g Fat,2.3g Carbs,44.1g Protei.

Hot Chicken Drumettes

Servings: 4
Cooking Time: 25 Minutes
Ingredients:
- 1 ½ pounds chicken drumettes
- 1/4 cup butter, melted
- A few dashes Tabasco
- Sea salt and red pepper flakes, to taste

Directions:
1. Select the "Air Fry" function and adjust the temperature to 375 degrees F. Press the "Start" key.
2. Place a sheet of parchment paper in the air fryer oven pan. Toss the chicken drumettes with the remaining ingredients.
3. Arrange the chicken drumettes in a single layer in the air fryer oven perforated pan.
4. Air fry the chicken drumettes for 10 minutes; turn them over and air fry for a further 10 minutes or until they are browned and crunchy.
5. Bon appétit!

Nutrition:
- Info472 Calories,38.6g Fat,1.4g Carbs,28.2g Protei.

Classic Chicken Drumsticks

Servings: 4
Cooking Time: 30 Minutes
Ingredients:

- 1 ½ pounds chicken drumsticks
- 2 tablespoon olive oil
- 1 teaspoon brown sugar
- 1 teaspoon paprika
- 1 teaspoon onion powder
- 1 teaspoon garlic powder
- Sea salt and ground black pepper, to taste

Directions:

1. Select the "Air Fry" function and adjust the temperature to 400 degrees F. Press the "Start" key.
2. Lightly grease the air fryer oven perforated pan with olive oil.
3. Toss the chicken drumsticks with the remaining ingredients.
4. When the display indicates "Add Food", place the drumsticks in the air fryer oven perforated pan.
5. Roast the chicken drumsticks for about 25 minutes, flipping them halfway through cooking.
6. Bon appétit!

Nutrition:

- Info419 Calories,26.3g Fat,2.2g Carbs,43.9g Protei.

Classic Chicken Tacos

Servings: 4
Cooking Time: 20 Minutes
Ingredients:

- 1 ½ pounds boneless skinless chicken breasts, cut into strips
- 2 tablespoons olive oil
- 1 teaspoon red chili powder
- Sea salt and coarse ground black pepper, to taste
- 1 teaspoon garlic, minced
- 1 teaspoon onion powder
- 1 teaspoon smoked paprika
- 1 lime, freshly squeezed
- 4 large tortillas
- 1/2 cup salsa

Directions:

1. Select the "Roast" function and adjust the temperature to 380 degrees F. Press the "Start" key.
2. Toss the chicken strips with olive oil, chili powder, salt, black pepper, garlic, onion powder, paprika, and lime juice.
3. Place the chicken in a baking pan.
4. When the display indicates "Add Food", place the baking pan on the cooking tray.
5. Roast the chicken for 15 minutes or until it reaches an internal temperature of 165 degrees F on a meat thermometer.
6. Assemble your tacos with tortillas and salsa, and serve immediately.

Nutrition:

- Info420 Calories,14.2g Fat,28.5g Carbs,42.7g Protei.

Bbq Chicken Legs

Servings: 4
Cooking Time: 30 Minutes
Ingredients:

- 1 ½ pounds chicken drumsticks
- 2 tablespoons olive oil
- 1 teaspoon garlic, pressed
- 1 teaspoon paprika
- Sea salt and ground black pepper, to taste
- 1/2 cup BBQ sauce

Directions:

1. Select the "Air Fry" function and adjust the temperature to 400 degrees F. Press the "Start" key.
2. Lightly grease the air fryer oven perforated pan with olive oil.
3. Toss the chicken legs with the remaining ingredients.
4. When the display indicates "Add Food", place the chicken legs in the air fryer oven perforated pan.
5. Roast the chicken legs for about 15 minutes; turn them over and continue cooking for an additional 10 minutes. You can cook them on the "Broil" function in the last 5 minutes if desired.
6. Bon appétit!

Nutrition:

- Info427 Calories,26.4g Fat,3.9g Carbs,44.3g Protei.

Creamed Chicken Salad

Servings: 4

Cooking Time: 20 Minutes

Ingredients:

- 1 ½ pounds boneless, skinless chicken breasts, cut into bite-sized chunks
- 1 teaspoon olive oil
- Salad:
- 2 stalks celery, chopped
- 1 bell pepper, seeded and chopped
- 1/2 cup Kalamata olives, pitted and sliced
- 1 small onion, chopped
- 1 small head Romaine lettuce, torn into pieces
- Dressing:
- 6 tablespoons mayonnaise
- 2 tablespoons sour cream
- 1 teaspoon white vinegar
- 1 teaspoon Dijon mustard
- Sea salt and ground black pepper, to taste

Directions:

1. Select the "Roast" function and adjust the temperature to 380 degrees F. Press the "Start" key.

2. Toss the chicken chunks with olive oil until well coated on all sides. Place the chicken in a baking pan.

3. When the display indicates "Add Food", place the baking pan on the cooking tray.

4. Roast the chicken in the preheated air fryer oven for 15 minutes or until cooked through.

5. Toss the chicken with the remaining salad ingredients. Mix all the dressing ingredients until well combined. Dress your salad and enjoy!

Nutrition:

- Info441 Calories,27.1g Fat,10.3g Carbs,39.6g Protei.

Turkey And Mushroom Croquettes

Servings: 5

Cooking Time: 20 Minutes

Ingredients:

- 1 pound ground chicken
- 4 ounces brown mushrooms, chopped
- 1/4 cup whole milk
- 2 medium eggs, beaten
- 1 small onion, chopped
- 1 cup breadcrumbs
- 1 tablespoon butter
- 1 tablespoon olive oil

Directions:

1. Select the "Air Fry" function and adjust the temperature to 350 degrees F. Press the "Start" key.

2. Place a sheet of parchment paper in the air fryer oven pan.

3. In a mixing bowl, thoroughly combine all the ingredients. Then, drop rounds of the mixture in a single layer onto the prepared pan using a small scoop.

4. Air fry the croquettes for 10 minutes; turn the croquettes over and increase the temperature to 400 degrees F. Air fry for a further 5 minutes to brown the outsides of the croquettes.

5. Bon appétit!

Nutrition:

- Info288 Calories,15.8g Fat,13.3g Carbs,21.1g Protei.

Chicken Fajita Salad

Servings: 4

Cooking Time: 20 Minutes + Chilling Time

Ingredients:

- 1 pound chicken breasts, cut into strips
- 1 tablespoon olive oil
- 2 tablespoons fresh lemon juice
- 1 celery stalk, chopped
- 1 small onions onion, chopped
- 1/2 cup mayonnaise
- Kosher salt and freshly ground black pepper, to taste
- 2 cups Romaine lettuce leaves, torn into pieces

Directions:

1. Select the "Roast" function and adjust the temperature to 380 degrees F. Press the "Start" key.

2. Place a sheet of parchment paper in the air fryer oven pan.

3. Toss the chicken strips with olive oil. When the display indicates "Add Food", place the chicken on the prepared air fryer oven pan.

4. Roast the chicken in the preheated air fryer oven for 15 minutes or until the chicken reaches an internal temperature of 165 degrees F on a meat thermometer.
5. Toss the chicken strips with the remaining ingredients and transfer your salad to the refrigerator until ready to serve.
6. Enjoy!

Nutrition:
- Info470 Calories,41.1g Fat,3.9g Carbs,21.8g Protei.

Authentic Chicken Fajitas

Servings: 4
Cooking Time: 20 Minutes
Ingredients:
- 1 pound boneless, skinless chicken breasts, cut into strips
- 2 tablespoons olive oil
- 1 teaspoon Dijon mustard
- 2 bell peppers, seeded and sliced
- 2 garlic cloves, sliced
- 1 teaspoon ground cumin
- Sea salt and ground black pepper, to taste
- 1 teaspoon chili powder
- 1 red onion, cut into wedges
- 4 whole-wheat tortillas

Directions:
1. Select the "Roast" function and adjust the temperature to 380 degrees F. Press the "Start" key.
2. Toss the chicken strips with olive oil, mustard, bell peppers, garlic, cumin, salt, black pepper, and chili powder.
3. Place the chicken and peppers in a baking pan. Place aluminum foil onto the drip pan.
4. When the display indicates "Add Food", place the baking pan on the cooking tray.
5. Roast the chicken and peppers in the preheated air fryer oven for 15 minutes or until the chicken reaches an internal temperature of 165 degrees F on a meat thermometer.
6. Assemble your fajitas with onion wedges and tortillas. Enjoy!

Nutrition:
- Info413 Calories,21.6g Fat,25.7g Carbs,28.8g Protei.

Mediterranean Chicken Salad

Servings: 4
Cooking Time: 45 Minutes
Ingredients:
- 1 ½ pounds skinless, boneless chicken breasts
- 3 tablespoons olive oil
- 2 tablespoons freshly squeezed lemon juice
- 1 tablespoon white vinegar
- 1 teaspoon yellow mustard
- 2 tablespoons fresh cilantro, chopped
- 2 tablespoons fresh basil, chopped
- 1 teaspoon dried oregano
- 2 garlic cloves, pressed
- 1 bell pepper, seeded and diced
- Sea salt and ground black pepper, to taste
- 2 cups Romaine lettuce leaves, torn into leaves
- 1 cucumber, diced
- 1 cup cherry tomatoes, halved
- 1 red onion, thinly sliced
- 3 ounces Kalamata olives pitted and sliced

Directions:
1. Select the "Roast" function and adjust the temperature to 360 degrees F. Press the "Start" key.
2. When the display indicates "Add Food", place the chicken in the parchment-lined air fryer oven pan.
3. Roast the chicken for about 20 minutes; flip it over and cook for 20 minutes longer or until the chicken reaches an internal temperature of 160 degrees F on a meat thermometer.
4. Transfer the chicken breast to a cutting board and let it rest for 10 minutes before slicing into strips.
5. Toss the chicken strips with the remaining ingredients and place your salad in the refrigerator until ready to serve. Bon appétit!

Nutrition:
- Info475 Calories,32g Fat,11.8g Carbs,36.6g Protei.

Chicken Sausage With Peppers

Servings: 4

Cooking Time: 15 Minutes

Ingredients:

- 1 pound chicken sausage, sliced
- 4 bell peppers, sliced
- 1 teaspoon garlic powder
- 2 tablespoons olive oil
- 1 teaspoon Italian seasoning mix
- Kosher salt and freshly ground black pepper, to taste

Directions:

1. Select the "Air Fry" function and adjust the temperature to 400 degrees F. Press the "Start" key.

2. Toss the chicken sausage and peppers with the remaining ingredients. Line the air fryer oven perforated pan with a sheet of parchment paper.

3. When the display indicates "Add Food", place the chicken sausage and peppers in the air fryer oven perforated pan.

4. Air fry the sausage and peppers for about 5 minutes; toss the pan and cook for 5 to 7 minutes longer or until cooked through.

5. Bon appétit!

Nutrition:

- Info340 Calories,27.3g Fat,4.8g Carbs,18.1g Protei.

Traditional Moroccan Brochettes

Servings: 4

Cooking Time: 25 Minutes

Ingredients:

- 1 pound skinless, boneless chicken breasts, cut into bite-sized pieces
- 1 teaspoon paprika
- Kosher salt and ground black pepper, to taste
- 1 teaspoon mustard seeds
- 1/2 teaspoon turmeric powder
- 2 tablespoons olive oil
- 8 bamboo or metal skewers

Directions:

1. Select the "Roast" function and adjust the temperature to 360 degrees F. Press the "Start" key.

2. Lightly grease the air fryer oven perforated pan with olive oil.

3. Toss all the ingredients in a mixing bowl. Thread the chicken pieces onto the skewers.

4. When the display indicates "Add Food", place the skewers in the air fryer oven perforated pan. Roast the skewers for about 20 minutes, rotating them once or twice.

5. Bon appétit!

Nutrition:

- Info267 Calories,17.5g Fat,1.5g Carbs,24g Protei.

Vegetables And Side Dishes Recipes

Italian-style Mushroom Patties

Servings: 4

Cooking Time: 15 Minutes

Ingredients:

- 1 pound Cremini mushrooms, chopped
- 1 small onion, chopped
- 2 garlic cloves, minced
- 1 bell pepper, chopped
- 2 tablespoons parsley, chopped
- 2 tablespoons cilantro, chopped
- 2 large eggs, beaten
- 1/2 cup breadcrumbs
- 1 tablespoon Italian seasoning mix
- 1 tablespoons soy sauce
- 2 teaspoon olive oil

Directions:

1. Select the "Air Fry" function and adjust the temperature to 390 degrees F. Press the "Start" key.
2. Place a sheet of parchment paper in the air fryer oven pan. Thoroughly combine all the ingredients.
3. Form the mixture into equal balls and place them in a single layer in the air fryer oven perforated pan.
4. Air fry the patties for 10 minutes, turning them over halfway through the cooking time.
5. Bon appétit!

Nutrition:

- Info139 Calories,5.7g Fat,13.4g Carbs,7.4g Protei.

Roasted Pepper And Cheese Bowl

Servings: 4

Cooking Time: 20 Minutes

Ingredients:

- 4 large bell peppers
- 2 tablespoons of olive oil
- Sea salt and ground black pepper, to taste
- 1 teaspoon garlic, minced
- 1 teaspoon dill weed

- 1 teaspoon Dijon mustard
- 2 tablespoons lemon juice
- 2 ounces feta cheese, crumbled

Directions:

1. Toss all the ingredients in a mixing bowl.
2. Select the "Air Fry" function and adjust the temperature to 400 degrees F. Press the "Start" key.
3. Arrange the peppers on the air fryer oven perforated pan, making sure not to crowd them.
4. Air fry the peppers for 15 minutes or until they're browned, shaking the pan once or twice during cooking.
5. Toss the peppers with the other ingredients. Bon appétit!

Nutrition:

- Info139 Calories,10.1g Fat,10.4g Carbs,3.8g Protei.

Grandma's Roasted Squash

Servings: 4

Cooking Time: 15 Minutes

Ingredients:

- 1 pound butternut squash, cut into 1/2-inch chunks
- 2 tablespoons coconut oil
- 2 tablespoons pure maple syrup
- A pinch of kosher salt
- A pinch of grated nutmeg
- 1/2 teaspoon ground cinnamon
- 1/2 teaspoon ground cloves

Directions:

1. Toss all the ingredients in a mixing bowl.
2. Select the "Roast" function and adjust the temperature to 380 degrees F. Press the "Start" key.
3. Arrange your squash on the parchment-lined air fryer oven perforated pan.
4. Air fry your squash for 12 minutes or until tender and cooked through.
5. Bon appétit!

Nutrition:
- Info133 Calories,6.9g Fat,18.7g Carbs,0.9g Protei.

Cheese-stuffed Mushrooms

Servings: 4
Cooking Time: 15 Minutes
Ingredients:
- 12 button mushrooms, washed
- 1 tablespoon olive oil
- 2 garlic cloves, minced
- 1/2 cup Parmesan cheese, grated
- 4 tablespoons tortilla chips, crushed
- Sea salt and ground black pepper, to taste
- 1/2 teaspoon mustard powder
- 1/2 teaspoon onion powder

Directions:
1. Pat the mushrooms dry and remove the stalks.
2. In a mixing bowl, thoroughly combine the remaining ingredients. Divide the filling between the prepared mushrooms.
3. Select the "Air Fry" function and adjust the temperature to 360 degrees F. Press the "Start" key.
4. Arrange the mushrooms on the air fryer oven perforated pan, making sure not to crowd them.
5. Air fry the mushrooms for 9 minutes or until cooked through.
6. Bon appétit!

Nutrition:
- Info239 Calories,9.8g Fat,29.4g Carbs,9.3g Protei.

Spicy Green Beans With Mushrooms

Servings: 4
Cooking Time: 15 Minutes
Ingredients:
- 1 pound fresh green beans, trimmed
- 1/2 pound button mushrooms, sliced
- 1 tablespoon sesame oil
- 1 tablespoons soy sauce
- 1 teaspoon rice wine vinegar

- 2 cloves garlic, pressed
- A few dashes of hot sauce

Directions:
1. Toss the green beans and mushrooms with the other ingredients in a mixing bowl.
2. Select the "Air Fry" function and adjust the temperature to 400 degrees F. Press the "Start" key.
3. Arrange the green beans and mushrooms on the parchment-lined air fryer oven perforated pan.
4. Air fry the green beans and mushrooms for 10 minutes. Serve immediately!

Nutrition:
- Info98 Calories,4.5g Fat,11.2g Carbs,4.2g Protei.

Golden Dijon Potatoes

Servings: 4
Cooking Time: 40 Minutes
Ingredients:
- 1 ½ pounds potatoes, peeled and diced
- 1/2 cup mayonnaise
- Coarse sea salt and freshly ground black pepper, to season
- 1 teaspoon lemon zest
- 1 tablespoon lemon juice
- 2 cloves garlic, minced
- 1 tablespoon Dijon mustard

Directions:
1. Toss all the ingredients in a mixing bowl.
2. Select the "Roast" function and adjust the temperature to 380 degrees F. Press the "Start" key.
3. Arrange your potatoes on the parchment-lined air fryer oven perforated pan.
4. Roast your potatoes for 35 minutes or until tender and cooked through. Serve warm and enjoy!

Nutrition:
- Info324 Calories,20.8g Fat,30.9g Carbs,4g Protei.

Cheesy Roasted Parsnips

Servings: 4

Cooking Time: 25 Minutes

Ingredients:

- 1 ½ pounds parsnips, sliced into 1/2-inch chunks
- 4 tablespoons butter
- 4 cloves garlic, pressed
- Kosher salt and freshly ground black pepper, to taste
- 1 teaspoon red pepper flakes, crushed
- 4 ounces cheddar cheese, grated

Directions:

1. Toss the parsnip, butter, garlic, and spices in a mixing bowl.
2. Select the "Air Fry" function and adjust the temperature to 380 degrees F. Press the "Start" key.
3. Arrange your parsnip on the parchment-lined air fryer oven perforated pan.
4. Air fry your parsnip for 15 minutes or until tender and cooked through. Top the parsnips with cheese and select the "Broil" function.
5. Continue baking for a further 5 minutes or until the cheese melts and browns slightly. Serve warm and enjoy!

Nutrition:

- Info349 Calories,21.6g Fat,32.1g Carbs,9.2g Protei.

Fried Breaded Portobellas

Servings: 4

Cooking Time: 15 Minutes

Ingredients:

- 3 medium eggs
- 1 teaspoon stone-ground mustard
- 1 tablespoon soy sauce
- 1/2 cup all-purpose flour
- 1 cup seasoned breadcrumbs
- 1 teaspoon smoked paprika
- Sea salt and ground black pepper, to taste
- 1 tablespoon olive oil
- 1 pound Portobello mushrooms

Directions:

1. In a shallow bowl, mix the egg, mustard, soy sauce, and flour. In another shallow bowl, place the breadcrumbs, spices, and olive oil.
2. Dredge the mushrooms in the egg mixture. Then, dip the mushrooms in the breadcrumb mixture, coating them completely.
3. Select the "Air Fry" function and adjust the temperature to 360 degrees F. Press the "Start" key.
4. Arrange the mushrooms on the air fryer oven perforated pan, making sure not to crowd them. Air fry the mushrooms for 10 minutes or until golden brown.
5. Bon appétit!

Nutrition:

- Info289 Calories,8g Fat,38.7g Carbs,10.4g Protei.

Roasted Buttery Eggplant

Servings: 4

Cooking Time: 25 Minutes

Ingredients:

- 1 pound eggplant, cut into 1 ½ -inch pieces
- 2 tablespoons butter, melted
- 1 tablespoon olive oil
- 1/2 teaspoon onion powder
- 1/4 teaspoon cumin, ground
- 1 teaspoon garlic powder
- 1/2 teaspoon ancho chile powder

Directions:

1. Toss all the ingredients in a mixing bowl.
2. Select the "Air Fry" function and adjust the temperature to 380 degrees F. Press the "Start" key.
3. Arrange eggplant pieces on the parchment-lined air fryer oven perforated pan.
4. Air fry the eggplant pieces for 20 minutes or until tender and cooked through.
5. Bon appétit!

Nutrition:

- Info115 Calories,9.3g Fat,7.6g Carbs,1.4g Protei.

Rainbow Beet Salad

Servings: 4

Cooking Time: 25 Minutes

Ingredients:

- 1 pound raw beet, peeled and cut into bite-sized pieces
- 1 teaspoon olive oil
- 2 tablespoons almonds, slivered
- 2 tablespoons pumpkin seeds, roasted
- 1 medium carrot, trimmed and julienned
- 2 cups arugula
- Vinaigrette:
- 2 tablespoons apple cider vinegar
- 1 tablespoon lime juice
- 4 tablespoons extra-virgin olive oil
- 2 tablespoons honey
- 1 teaspoon Dijon mustard
- Kosher salt and freshly cracked black pepper, to taste

Directions:

1. Toss the beets with 1 teaspoon of olive oil until well coated.
2. Select the "Air Fry" function and adjust the temperature to 400 degrees F. Press the "Start" key.
3. Arrange the beets on the air fryer oven perforated pan. Air fry the beets for 20 minutes, shaking the pan once or twice during cooking.
4. Toss the roasted beets with almonds, pumpkin seeds, carrot, and arugula. Then, in a small bowl, whisk all the vinaigrette ingredients.
5. Dress your salad and serve immediately. Enjoy!

Nutrition:

- Info281 Calories,20g Fat,23.7g Carbs,4.8g Protei.

Roasted Brussels Sprouts

Servings: 4

Cooking Time: 15 Minutes

Ingredients:

- 1 ½ pounds Brussels sprouts, trimmed and halved
- 2 tablespoons butter, melted
- 1 teaspoon cayenne pepper
- 1/2 teaspoon dried thyme
- 1 teaspoon dried parsley flakes
- Sea salt and ground black pepper, to taste

Directions:

1. Toss the Brussels sprouts with the remaining ingredients in a mixing bowl.
2. Select the "Air Fry" function and adjust the temperature to 375 degrees F. Press the "Start" key.
3. Arrange the Brussels sprouts on the parchment-lined air fryer oven perforated pan. Bake Brussels sprouts for 5 minutes.
4. Increase the heat to 400 degrees F. Give the pan a good shake and continue to cook for another 8 minutes or until tender.
5. Bon appétit!

Nutrition:

- Info128 Calories,6.3g Fat,15.5g Carbs,6g Protei.

Roasted Baby Potatoes

Servings: 4

Cooking Time: 35 Minutes

Ingredients:

- 1 ½ pounds baby potatoes, scrubbed and halved
- 1 tablespoon fresh lemon juice
- 2 tablespoons olive oil
- 1 teaspoon garlic powder
- 1 teaspoon onion powder
- 1 teaspoon Italian seasoning mix
- Kosher salt and ground black pepper, to taste

Directions:

1. Toss the baby potatoes with the remaining ingredients in a mixing bowl.
2. Select the "Air Fry" function and adjust the temperature to 400 degrees F. Press the "Start" key.
3. Arrange the baby potatoes on the parchment-lined air fryer oven perforated pan. Bake the baby potatoes for 30 minutes, turning them over halfway through.
4. Bon appétit!

Nutrition:

- Info188 Calories,7.1g Fat,28.7g Carbs,3.6g Protei.

Roasted Sweet Potatoes

Servings: 4
Cooking Time: 40 Minutes
Ingredients:
- 1 pound sweet potatoes, peeled and diced
- 2 teaspoons olive oil
- 1 teaspoon cayenne pepper
- 1/2 teaspoon dried dill weed
- Sea salt and freshly ground black pepper, to taste

Directions:
1. Toss all the ingredients in a mixing bowl.
2. Select the "Roast" function and adjust the temperature to 380 degrees F. Press the "Start" key.
3. Arrange your sweet potatoes on the parchment-lined air fryer oven perforated pan.
4. Roast your sweet potatoes for 35 minutes or until tender and cooked through.
5. Bon appétit!

Nutrition:
- Info119 Calories,2.3g Fat,23.1g Carbs,1.9g Protei.

Roasted Pepper Salad

Servings: 4
Cooking Time: 20 Minutes
Ingredients:
- 4 large bell peppers
- 2 tablespoons olive oil
- 2 tablespoons apple cider vinegar
- Sea salt and ground black pepper, to taste
- 2 garlic cloves, crushed
- 2 tablespoons fresh parsley, chopped
- 2 tablespoons fresh scallions, chopped

Directions:
1. Toss all the ingredients in a mixing bowl.
2. Select the "Air Fry" function and adjust the temperature to 400 degrees F. Press the "Start" key.
3. Arrange the peppers on the air fryer oven perforated pan, making sure not to crowd them.
4. Air fry the peppers for 15 minutes or until they're browned, shaking the pan once or twice during cooking.

5. Peel away the browned outer layer, if desired; cut the peppers into strips and add in the remaining ingredients.
6. Toss to combine and serve well-chilled. Enjoy!

Nutrition:
- Info119 Calories,7.3g Fat,11.7g Carbs,2g Protei.

Herbed Roasted Zucchini

Servings: 4
Cooking Time: 20 Minutes
Ingredients:
- 1 pound zucchini, quartered lengthwise
- 1 tablespoon Italian seasoning
- Coarse sea salt and ground black pepper, to taste
- 4 tablespoons extra-virgin olive oil
- 2 tablespoons freshly squeezed lemon juice
- 1 teaspoon Dijon mustard
- 2 tablespoons fresh parsley, chopped
- 2 tablespoons fresh basil, chopped
- 1 tablespoon fresh mint, chopped

Directions:
1. Toss all the ingredients in a mixing bowl.
2. Select the "Air Fry" function and adjust the temperature to 400 degrees F. Press the "Start" key.
3. Arrange the zucchini on the parchment-lined air fryer oven perforated pan.
4. Roast the zucchini for 15 minutes or until tender and cooked through.
5. Bon appétit!

Nutrition:
- Info158 Calories,14.6g Fat,6.6g Carbs,2.1g Protei.

Lemon-herb Sweet Potatoes

Servings: 4
Cooking Time: 40 Minutes
Ingredients:

- 1 small onion, finely chopped
- 1 tablespoon grated lemon zest
- 1 tablespoon fresh lemon juice
- 1 ½ pounds sweet potatoes, peeled and diced
- 2 tablespoons butter, melted
- Kosher salt and ground black pepper, to taste
- 1 jalapeno pepper, seeded and chopped
- 1 tablespoon fresh mint, chopped
- 2 tablespoon fresh chives, chopped
- 2 tablespoons fresh parsley, chopped

Directions:

1. Toss all the ingredients in a mixing bowl.
2. Select the "Roast" function and adjust the temperature to 380 degrees F. Press the "Start" key.
3. Arrange your sweet potatoes on the parchment-lined air fryer oven perforated pan.
4. Roast your sweet potatoes for 35 minutes or until tender and cooked through.
5. Bon appétit!

Nutrition:

- Info214 Calories,5.9g Fat,37.8g Carbs,3.3g Protei.

Parmesan Fennel Patties

Servings: 4
Cooking Time: 20 Minutes
Ingredients:

- 1 pound fennel, trimmed and chopped
- 1 small onion, chopped
- 2 garlic cloves, minced
- 2 eggs, whisked
- 1/2 cup parmesan cheese, grated
- 2 tablespoons chives, chopped
- 2 tablespoons parsley, chopped
- 1 teaspoon lemon zest
- Sea salt and ground black pepper, to taste
- 1 cup all-purpose flour
- 2 tablespoons olive oil

Directions:

1. Select the "Air Fry" function and adjust the temperature to 380 degrees F. Press the "Start" key.
2. Place a sheet of parchment paper in the air fryer oven pan. Thoroughly combine all the ingredients.
3. Form the mixture into four patties and place them in a single layer in the air fryer oven perforated pan.
4. Air fry the patties for 15 minutes, turning them over halfway through.
5. Bon appétit!

Nutrition:

- Info341 Calories,15.6g Fat,37.8g Carbs,13.3g Protei.

Buttery Roasted Carrots

Servings: 4
Cooking Time: 25 Minutes
Ingredients:

- 1 pound carrots, sliced lengthwise
- 2 teaspoons butter, melted
- 1 teaspoon cayenne pepper
- 1 teaspoon dried oregano
- Kosher salt and ground black pepper, to taste

Directions:

1. Toss all the ingredients in a mixing bowl.
2. Select the "Air Fry" function and adjust the temperature to 380 degrees F. Press the "Start" key.
3. Arrange your carrots on the parchment-lined air fryer oven perforated pan.
4. Air fry your carrots for 20 minutes or until tender and cooked through.
5. Bon appétit!

Nutrition:

- Info66 Calories,2.4g Fat,11.2g Carbs,1.6g Protei.

Herb And Garlic Potatoes

Servings: 4

Cooking Time: 40 Minutes

Ingredients:

- 1 ½ pound potatoes, peeled and diced
- 3 tablespoons olive oil
- 1 tablespoon butter, softened
- Coarse sea salt and ground black pepper, to taste
- 1 teaspoon smoked paprika
- 1 teaspoon garlic, minced
- 1 teaspoon rosemary, chopped
- 1 teaspoon thyme, chopped

Directions:

1. Toss all the ingredients in a mixing bowl.
2. Select the "Roast" function and adjust the temperature to 380 degrees F. Press the "Start" key.
3. Arrange your potatoes on the parchment-lined air fryer oven perforated pan.
4. Roast your potatoes for 35 minutes or until tender and cooked through. Serve warm and enjoy!

Nutrition:

- Info254 Calories,13.5g Fat,31.4g Carbs,3.8g Protei.

Cheesy Butternut Squash

Servings: 4

Cooking Time: 15 Minutes

Ingredients:

- 1 ½ pounds butternut squash, cut into 1/2-inch chunks
- 2 tablespoons extra-virgin olive oil
- 1 teaspoon lemon zest
- A pinch of grated nutmeg
- Kosher salt and cayenne pepper, to taste
- 4 ounces Parmesan cheese, grated

Directions:

1. Toss all the ingredients in a mixing bowl.
2. Select the "Roast" function and adjust the temperature to 380 degrees F. Press the "Start" key.
3. Arrange your squash on the parchment-lined air fryer oven perforated pan.
4. Roast your squash for 12 minutes or until tender and cooked through.
5. Bon appétit!

Nutrition:

- Info260 Calories,14.6g Fat,24.4g Carbs,9.9g Protei.

Vegan Recipes

Spicy Creamed Beet Salad

Servings: 4
Cooking Time: 25 Minutes
Ingredients:

- 1 pound red beets, scrubbed and diced
- 1 tablespoon olive oil
- Kosher salt and ground black pepper, to season
- 1/2 cup vegan mayonnaise
- 1 tablespoon yellow mustard
- 1/2 teaspoon ground bay leaf
- 1 red bell pepper, seeded and sliced
- 1 small chili pepper, seeded and chopped

Directions:

1. Toss the golden beets with 1 tablespoon of olive oil in a mixing bowl.
2. Select the "Air Fry" function and adjust the temperature to 400 degrees F. Press the "Start" key.
3. Arrange the beets on the air fryer oven perforated pan, making sure not to crowd them.
4. Air fry the beets for 20 minutes or until they're browned, shaking the pan once or twice during cooking.
5. Toss the roasted beets with the remaining ingredients and serve at room temperature.
6. Bon appétit!

Nutrition:

- Info284 Calories,24.3g Fat,14.4g Carbs,3g Protei.

Smoked Tempeh Sandwich

Servings: 3
Cooking Time: 25 Minutes
Ingredients:

- 9 ounces tempeh, sliced
- 1 tablespoon Dijon mustard
- 2 tablespoons soy sauce
- 2 tablespoons red wine vinegar
- 2 tablespoons tomato paste
- 1 garlic clove, pressed
- 2 scallion stalks, chopped
- 1 teaspoon smoked paprika
- 6 slices whole-grain bread

Directions:

1. In a ceramic bowl, thoroughly combine all the ingredients, except for the bread. Cover and let it marinate for about 1 hour.
2. Select the "Air Fry" function and adjust the temperature to 395 degrees F. Press the "Start" key.
3. Arrange the tempeh slice on the air fryer oven perforated pan, making sure not to crowd them. Reserve the marinade.
4. Air fry the tempeh slices for 10 minutes. Flip the tempeh slices and baste them with the reserved marinade; continue to cook for 10 minutes longer or until golden brown.
5. Assemble your sandwiches with bread slices and roasted tempeh; serve immediately and enjoy!

Nutrition:

- Info451 Calories,15.2g Fat,53.2g Carbs,30.5g Protei.

Roasted Golden Beets

Servings: 4
Cooking Time: 25 Minutes
Ingredients:

- 1 pound golden beets, scrubbed and diced
- 1/4 cup olive oil
- 2 tablespoons apple cider vinegar
- Coarse sea salt and ground black pepper, to taste
- 1/2 teaspoon ground cumin
- 1 tablespoon Dijon mustard

Directions:

1. Toss the golden beets with 1 tablespoon of olive oil in a mixing bowl.
2. Select the "Air Fry" function and adjust the temperature to 400 degrees F. Press the "Start" key.

3.   Arrange the beets on the air fryer oven perforated pan, making sure not to crowd them.

4.   Air fry the beets for 20 minutes or until they're browned, shaking the pan once or twice during cooking.

5.   Toss the roasted beets with the remaining ingredients and serve at room temperature.

6.   Bon appétit!

Nutrition:
- Info179 Calories,13.9g Fat,12.3g Carbs,2.3g Protei.

Rosemary Roasted Potatoes

Servings: 4
Cooking Time: 40 Minutes
Ingredients:
- 1 ½ pounds potatoes, peeled and cut into quarters
- 2 tablespoons olive oil
- Coarse sea salt and freshly ground black pepper, to taste
- 1 teaspoon cayenne pepper
- 1 tablespoon dried rosemary, minced

Directions:
1.   Select the "Air Fry" function and adjust the temperature to 400 degrees F. Press the "Start" key.

2.   Toss the potato chunks with the remaining ingredients.

3.   When the display indicates "Add Food", place the potato chunks in the air fryer oven perforated pan.

4.   Air fry the potatoes for 35 minutes, turning them over at the halfway point.

5.   Bon appétit!

Nutrition:
- Info193 Calories,7.1g Fat,30.1g Carbs,3.5g Protei.

Cashew Oatmeal Muffins

Servings: 8
Cooking Time: 20 Minutes
Ingredients:
- 2 cups old-fashioned rolled oats
- 1 teaspoon baking powder
- 1/2 teaspoon baking soda

- 2 cups oat milk (or cashew milk)
- 1/2 cup cashew butter
- 2 bananas, mashed
- 1/4 cup agave syrup
- 1 teaspoon pure vanilla extract
- A pinch of kosher salt and grated nutmeg
- 1 teaspoon ground cinnamon

Directions:
1.   Select the "Air Fry" function and adjust the temperature to 390 degrees F. Press the "Start" key.

2.   Thoroughly combine all the ingredients. Spoon the mixture into lightly greased muffin cups.

3.   Air fry the oatmeal cups for 15 minutes or until golden brown.

4.   Bon appétit!

Nutrition:
- Info229 Calories,15.2g Fat,27g Carbs,6.1g Protei.

Mediterranean-style Fingerling Potatoes

Servings: 4
Cooking Time: 35 Minutes
Ingredients:
- 1 ½ pounds fingerling potatoes, scrubbed
- 2 tablespoons olive oil
- 1 teaspoon garlic powder
- 1 tablespoon fresh parsley, chopped
- 2 teaspoons fresh thyme, chopped
- 1 teaspoon red pepper flakes, crushed
- Sea salt and ground black pepper, to taste

Directions:
1.   Toss the fingerling potatoes with the remaining ingredients in a mixing bowl.

2.   Select the "Air Fry" function and adjust the temperature to 400 degrees F. Press the "Start" key.

3.   Arrange the fingerling potatoes on the parchment-lined air fryer oven perforated pan. Bake the fingerling potatoes for 30 minutes, turning them over halfway through.

4.   Bon appétit!

Nutrition:

- Info197 Calories,6.9g Fat,30.4g Carbs,3.6g Protei.

Italian-style Eggplant

Servings: 4
Cooking Time: 20 Minutes
Ingredients:

- 1 pound eggplant, sliced
- 1 teaspoon garlic powder
- 1 teaspoon onion powder
- 1 teaspoon hot paprika
- Kosher salt and ground black pepper, to taste
- 1/4 teaspoon ground cumin
- 2 tablespoons olive oil
- 1/2 cup marinara sauce

Directions:

1. In a mixing bowl, toss the eggplant with the spices and olive oil.
2. Select the "Air Fry" function and adjust the temperature to 390 degrees F. Press the "Start" key.
3. Place the eggplant on the parchment-lined air fryer oven perforated pan.
4. Roast the eggplant for 10 minutes. Top them with marinara sauce; continue to cook for a further 5 minutes.
5. Bon appétit!

Nutrition:

- Info109 Calories,7.1g Fat,11.3g Carbs,2.1g Protei.

Fried Broccoli Florets

Servings: 4
Cooking Time: 10 Minutes
Ingredients:

- 1 pound broccoli florets
- 2 teaspoons olive oil
- 2 teaspoons tahini
- 1 tablespoon nutritional yeast
- 1/2 teaspoon garlic powder
- 1/2 teaspoon onion powder
- Kosher salt and cayenne pepper, to taste

Directions:

1. Toss all the ingredients in a mixing bowl.
2. Select the "Air Fry" function and adjust the temperature to 400 degrees F. Press the "Start" key.
3. Arrange the broccoli florets on the air fryer oven perforated pan, making sure not to crowd them.
4. Air fry the broccoli florets for 6 minutes or until cooked through, tossing them once or twice during cooking time.
5. Bon appétit!

Nutrition:

- Info88 Calories,4.1g Fat,10.6g Carbs,5.1g Protei.

Fried Tofu With Sweet Potatoes

Servings: 5
Cooking Time: 35 Minutes
Ingredients:

- 1 pound sweet potatoes, peeled and cut into 1-inch chunks
- 10 ounces extra-firm tofu, pressed and cut into 1-inch chunks
- 1 teaspoon garlic, minced
- 2 tablespoons scallions, chopped
- 1 teaspoon paprika - divided
- Kosher salt and ground black pepper, to taste
- 2 tablespoons cornstarch
- 2 tablespoons olive oil

Directions:

1. In a mixing bowl, thoroughly combine all the ingredients.
2. Select the "Air Fry" function and adjust the temperature to 395 degrees F. Press the "Start" key.
3. Arrange the sweet potatoes on the air fryer oven perforated pan, making sure not to crowd them.
4. Air fry the sweet potatoes for 20 minutes or until soft; make sure to toss them occasionally to ensure even cooking.
5. Add in the tofu cubes and continue cooking for a further 10 minutes or until cooked through.
6. Bon appétit!

Nutrition:

- Info188 Calories,8.8g Fat,21.4g Carbs,7.7g Protei.

Nutrition:
- Info277 Calories,5.3g Fat,46.4g Carbs,8.8g Protei.

Toasted Tortillas With Avocado

Servings: 2
Cooking Time: 10 Minutes
Ingredients:
- 2 whole-wheat tortillas
- 1/3 cup hummus
- 2 tablespoons tomato ketchup
- 1/2 avocado, pitted, peeled and sliced
- Handful fresh arugula

Directions:
1. Assemble taco wraps by filling each tortilla with equal amount of the rest of the ingredients.
2. Select the "Toast" function and press the "Start" key.
3. Toast your taco wraps for 3 minutes or so.
4. Serve immediately and enjoy!

Nutrition:
- Info297 Calories,15g Fat,33.5g Carbs,7.7g Protei.

Classic Toasted Sandwich

Servings: 1
Cooking Time: 10 Minutes
Ingredients:
- 4 slices bread
- 2 tablespoons hummus
- 1 small tomato, sliced
- 2 lettuce leaves

Directions:
1. Assemble your sandwich with hummus, tomato, and lettuce; you can use a toothpick to keep the sandwich together.
2. When the display indicates "Add Food", place the sandwich on the air fryer tray.
3. Select the "Toast" function and press the "Start" key.
4. Toast your sandwich for about 3 minutes or so. Serve immediately.

Italian-style Cremini Mushrooms

Servings: 4
Cooking Time: 15 Minutes
Ingredients:
- 1 pound Cremini mushrooms, sliced
- 1/2 cup flour
- 4 tablespoons vegan mayonnaise
- 1/4 cup cream of onion soup
- 1 cup breadcrumbs
- 1 teaspoon garlic powder
- 1 teaspoon onion powder
- 1 teaspoon hot paprika
- 1 teaspoon Italian seasoning
- Kosher salt and ground black pepper, to taste

Directions:
1. Pat the mushrooms dry.
2. In a mixing bowl, thoroughly combine all the remaining ingredients. Then, dip the mushrooms in the breadcrumb mixture, coating them on all sides.
3. Select the "Air Fry" function and adjust the temperature to 360 degrees F. Press the "Start" key.
4. Arrange the mushrooms on the air fryer oven perforated pan, making sure not to crowd them. Air fry the mushrooms for 10 minutes, giving the perforated pan a shake at five-minute intervals to ensure the tofu cooks evenly.
5. Bon appétit!

Nutrition:
- Info244 Calories,11.9g Fat,28.9g Carbs,5.1g Protei.

Cabbage Steaks With Tofu

Servings: 4

Cooking Time: 25 Minutes

Ingredients:

- 1 pound cabbage, cut into steaks
- 12 ounces tofu, crumbled
- 1/4 cup extra-virgin olive oil
- 2 cloves garlic, pressed
- 1 teaspoon cayenne pepper
- Kosher salt and ground black pepper, to taste
- 1 tablespoon fresh lemon juice

Directions:

1. Select the "Air Fry" function and adjust the temperature to 380 degrees F. Press the "Start" key.
2. Toss your cabbage with the remaining ingredients.
3. Air fry your cabbage and tofu for 20 minutes or until golden brown.
4. Bon appétit!

Nutrition:

- Info287 Calories,21.2g Fat,14.1g Carbs,15.4g Protei.

Kid-friendly Corn Muffins

Servings: 6

Cooking Time: 15 Minutes

Ingredients:

- 1 ½ cups all-purpose flour
- 1 cup cornmeal
- 1 teaspoon baking powder
- 1/2 teaspoon baking soda
- 1/2 cup creamed corn kernels
- 1/4 cup agave syrup
- 1 teaspoon salt
- 1/4 teaspoon grated nutmeg
- 1 cup almond milk
- 1/4 cup applesauce

Directions:

1. Select the "Bake" function and adjust the temperature to 390 degrees F. Press the "Start" key.
2. In a mixing bowl, stir together the dry ingredients. Then, in a separate bowl, thoroughly combine all the wet ingredients.
3. Add the wet mixture to the dry ingredients and stir just until moistened. Spoon the batter into a parchment-lined muffin tin.
4. Bake your muffins for 5 minutes. Reduce temperature to 330 degrees F and continue to bake for a further 7 minutes or until a tester comes out dry.
5. Bon appétit!

Nutrition:

- Info294 Calories,3.3g Fat,60.4g Carbs,7.5g Protei.

Autumn Pumpkin Pancakes

Servings: 4

Cooking Time: 15 Minutes

Ingredients:

- 1/3 cup pumpkin purée
- 1 cup coconut flour
- 1 teaspoon ground flax seeds
- 2 teaspoons brown sugar
- 1 teaspoon baking powder
- A pinch of kosher salt
- 1/2 cup coconut milk
- 2 teaspoons soy butter
- 1 teaspoon pumpkin pie spice mix

Directions:

1. In a mixing bowl, thoroughly combine the dry ingredients. In another bowl, whisk the wet ingredients. Add the wet mixture to the dry ingredients; mix to combine well.
2. Grease a baking pan with nonstick cooking oil and set it aside.
3. Select the "Air Fry" function and adjust the temperature to 350 degrees F. Press the "Start" key.
4. Cook your pancakes for about 13 minutes, working in batches, if needed. Enjoy!

Nutrition:

- Info121 Calories,9.8g Fat,7.1g Carbs,1.9g Protei.

Quinoa And Chickpea Meatballs

Servings: 4
Cooking Time: 20 Minutes
Ingredients:

- 1 cup cooked quinoa
- 12 ounces canned chickpeas, drained
- 2 tablespoons olive oil
- 1 small onion, chopped
- 2 cloves garlic, minced
- Sea salt and ground black pepper, to taste
- 1 teaspoon red pepper flakes, crushed
- 2 tablespoons tomato paste
- 1 tablespoon soy sauce

Directions:

1. Select the "Air Fry" function and adjust the temperature to 400 degrees F. Press the "Start" key.
2. Place a sheet of parchment paper in the air fryer oven pan.
3. Mix all the ingredients in your blender or food processor.
4. Form the mixture into equal balls and place them in a single layer in the air fryer oven perforated pan.
5. Air fry the balls for 15 minutes, shaking the pan to ensure even cooking. Serve immediately and enjoy!

Nutrition:

- Info268 Calories,10.8g Fat,34.1g Carbs,9.2g Protei.

Carrot Puree With Herbs

Servings: 4
Cooking Time: 25 Minutes
Ingredients:

- 1 pound carrots, trimmed and halved lengthwise
- 1 tablespoon olive oil
- 2 garlic cloves, minced
- 1/4 cup cream of celery soup
- 2 tablespoons tahini
- Sea salt and cayenne pepper, to taste
- 1 teaspoon red pepper flakes, crushed
- 1 tablespoon fresh parsley, chopped
- 1 tablespoon fresh cilantro, chopped
- 1 tablespoon fresh sage, chopped

Directions:

1. Toss the carrots with olive oil.
2. Select the "Air Fry" function and adjust the temperature to 380 degrees F. Press the "Start" key.
3. Arrange your carrots on the parchment-lined air fryer oven perforated pan.
4. Air fry your carrots for 20 minutes or until tender and cooked through.
5. Next, puree the roasted carrots with the garlic, soup, tahini, salt, and cayenne pepper until everything is well incorporated.
6. Garnish your puree with red pepper flakes and herbs. Bon appétit!

Nutrition:

- Info136 Calories,8.1g Fat,14.9g Carbs,2.9g Protei.

Roasted Garlic Cabbage

Servings: 4
Cooking Time: 20 Minutes
Ingredients:

- 1 pound green cabbage, cut into wedges
- 2 tablespoons olive oil
- Kosher salt and ground black pepper, to taste
- 2 garlic cloves, minced
- 1/2 teaspoon red pepper flakes
- 1 teaspoon celery seeds

Directions:

1. Select the "Air Fry" function and adjust the temperature to 380 degrees F. Press the "Start" key.
2. Toss your cabbage with the remaining ingredients.
3. Air fry your cabbage for 15 minutes or until golden brown. Serve hot and enjoy!

Nutrition:

- Info104 Calories,7.1g Fat,10.1g Carbs,2.1g Protei.

Crispy Breaded Mushrooms

Servings: 4

Cooking Time: 15 Minutes

Ingredients:

- 1 pound brown mushrooms
- 1/4 cup oat milk (or rice milk)
- 1 cup tortilla chips, crushed
- 2 teaspoon olive oil
- 2 garlic cloves, minced
- Sea salt and ground black pepper, to taste
- 1 teaspoon smoked paprika
- 2 tablespoons nutritional yeast

Directions:

1. Pat the mushrooms dry.
2. In a mixing bowl, thoroughly combine all the remaining ingredients. Then, dip the mushrooms in the breadcrumb mixture, coating them on all sides.
3. Select the "Air Fry" function and adjust the temperature to 360 degrees F. Press the "Start" key.
4. Arrange the mushrooms on the air fryer oven perforated pan, making sure not to crowd them. Air fry the mushrooms for 10 minutes or until golden brown.
5. Bon appétit!

Nutrition:

- Info243 Calories,10.7g Fat,30.1g Carbs,8.6g Protei.

Authentic Indian Kofta

Servings: 4

Cooking Time: 20 Minutes

Ingredients:

- 1 block firm tofu, pressed and crumbled
- 1/2 cup raw cashews, ground
- 1 large potato, boiled and mashed
- 1 green chili pepper, minced
- 1 teaspoon ginger-garlic paste
- 2 tablespoons cornstarch
- Sea salt and ground black pepper, to taste
- 2 teaspoons soy sauce
- 2 teaspoons sesame oil (or olive oil)

Directions:

1. Select the "Air Fry" function and adjust the temperature to 400 degrees F. Press the "Start" key.
2. Place a sheet of parchment paper in the air fryer oven pan. Thoroughly combine all the ingredients.
3. Form the mixture into equal balls and place them in a single layer in the air fryer oven perforated pan.
4. Air fry the balls for 15 minutes or until cooked through. Serve hot and enjoy!

Nutrition:

- Info494 Calories,30.8g Fat,36.6g Carbs,25.7g Protei.

Desserts Recipes

Peach Crumble Cake

Servings: 6
Cooking Time: 15 Minutes
Ingredients:

- 1/2 cup old-fashioned oats
- 1/4 cup almond meal
- 1/2 teaspoon baking powder
- A pinch of sea salt
- 1/4 cup butter, cold
- 3 large peaches, peeled, pitted and diced
- 1/2 teaspoon ground anise
- 1 teaspoon ginger, peeled and ground
- 1 teaspoon ground cinnamon
- 1/4 cup brown sugar
- 1 tablespoon honey

Directions:

1. Select the "Bake" function and adjust the temperature to 360 degrees F. Press the "Start" key.
2. Mix the oats, almond meal, baking powder, salt, and butter. Mix until smooth and uniform.
3. Press the mixture into a lightly greased baking pan. Toss the peaches with the remaining ingredients and place them on the crust.
4. Bake the crumble cake for approximately 12 minutes or until the topping is golden brown. Enjoy!

Nutrition:

- Info227 Calories,10.8g Fat,25.4g Carbs,4g Protei.

Vanilla Maple Apricots

Servings: 4
Cooking Time: 15 Minutes
Ingredients:

- 1 pound apricots, pitted and halved
- 4 tablespoons maple syrup
- 1/2 teaspoon vanilla extract
- 1/2 teaspoon ground cardamom
- 1/2 teaspoon ground cinnamon
- A pinch of grated nutmeg
- A pinch of kosher salt

Directions:

1. In a mixing bowl, thoroughly combine all the ingredients.
2. Select the "Air Fry" function and adjust the temperature to 350 degrees F. Press the "Start" key.
3. Bake the apricots for 10 to 11 minutes or until tender and lightly caramelized.
4. Serve at room temperature and enjoy!

Nutrition:

- Info111 Calories,0.5g Fat,26.5g Carbs,1.6g Protei.

Homemade Pâte à Choux

Servings: 6
Cooking Time: 1 Hour 20 Minutes
Ingredients:

- 2 tablespoons coconut oil, melted
- 2 tablespoons aquafaba
- 1 teaspoon vanilla extract
- 3 cups all-purpose flour
- 1/4 teaspoon ground cinnamon

Directions:

1. Select the "Air Fry" function and adjust the temperature to 360 degrees F. Press the "Start" key.
2. Using the paddle attachment, thoroughly combine the coconut oil, aquafaba, and vanilla. Now, slowly and gradually, add in the flour and cinnamon.
3. Knead the dough for approximately 3 minutes; cover the dough with a clean dish towel and let it rise for 1 hour in a warm place.
4. Roll out the dough and cut it into 24 squares.
5. Select the "Air Fry" function and adjust the temperature to 350 degrees F. Press the "Start" key.
6. Lower the squares into a lightly greased baking pan.
7. Air fry the squares at 340 degrees F for about 15 minutes or until golden brown, flipping them halfway through the cooking time.
8. Serve with toppings of choice and enjoy!

Nutrition:
- Info269 Calories,5.2g Fat,47.9g Carbs,6.5g Protei.

Vanilla And Honey-roasted Peaches

Servings: 4
Cooking Time: 15 Minutes
Ingredients:
- 4 teaspoons coconut oil
- 4 tablespoons honey
- 1 tablespoon rum
- 1 teaspoon pure vanilla extract
- 1/2 teaspoon ground anise
- 1/4 teaspoon kosher salt
- 4 large ripe peaches, pitted and halved
- 4 tablespoons Greek-style yogurt

Directions:
1. In a mixing bowl, thoroughly combine the coconut oil, honey, rum, vanilla, anise, and salt. Divide the filling between the peaches.
2. Select the "Roast" function and adjust the temperature to 350 degrees F. Press the "Start" key.
3. Bake the peaches for 12 minutes or until tender. Garnish the roasted peaches with Greek yogurt and serve at room temperature.
4. Enjoy!

Nutrition:
- Info194 Calories,5g Fat,34.8g Carbs,3.2g Protei.

Almond Energy Bars

Servings: 8
Cooking Time: 35 Minutes
Ingredients:
- 1 cup old-fashioned rolled oats
- 1 cup almond meal
- 1/2 cup brown sugar
- 2 tablespoons honey
- 1 ½ teaspoons baking powder
- 1/4 teaspoon salt
- 1/2 teaspoon ground cinnamon

- 1/2 cup peanut butter
- 1/2 cup almond milk
- 2 eggs
- 1 teaspoon vanilla extract
- 2 ounces dried cranberries

Directions:
1. Select the "Air Fry" function and adjust the temperature to 360 degrees F. Press the "Start" key.
2. In a large mixing bowl, stir together all the dry ingredients. In another bowl, mix the wet ingredients.
3. Add the wet mixture to the dry ingredients and stir to combine well. Fold in the cranberries.
4. Press the batter onto a parchment-lined baking pan. Bake the bars for approximately 15 minutes or until golden brown.
5. Let it sit on a wire rack for 20 minutes before slicing and serving.
6. Bon appétit!

Nutrition:
- Info285 Calories,11.8g Fat,37.1g Carbs,8.8g Protei.

Fluffy Almond Brownie Squares

Servings: 6
Cooking Time: 20 Minutes
Ingredients:
- 1/4 cup all-purpose flour
- 1/4 cup almond meal
- 2/3 cup granulated sugar
- 1/2 cup cocoa powder
- 1/2 teaspoon baking powder
- A pinch of kosher salt
- A pinch of grated nutmeg
- 1/3 cup coconut oil, melted
- 2 eggs, beaten

Directions:
1. Brush a baking pan with nonstick cooking spray oil; set it aside.
2. Mix the dry ingredients in a bowl; now, thoroughly combine the wet ingredients. Add the wet mixture to the dry mixture and mix until everything is well incorporated.

3. Select the "Bake" function and adjust the temperature to 330 degrees F. Press the "Start" key. When the display indicates "Add Food", place the baking pan on the air fryer tray.

4. Bake your brownie for 15 minutes or until a tester comes out clean when inserted in the middle.

5. Bon appétit!

Nutrition:
- Info277 Calories,16.3g Fat,33.2g Carbs,4.5g Protei.

Vanilla Walnut Blondies

Servings: 7
Cooking Time: 20 Minutes
Ingredients:
- 1 cup all-purpose flour
- 1/2 cup coconut flour
- 1 teaspoon baking powder
- 1 stick butter, melted
- 1/2 cup brown sugar
- 2 large eggs, well-beaten
- 1 teaspoon vanilla extract
- A pinch of grated nutmeg
- A pinch of kosher salt
- 1/2 cup walnuts, chopped

Directions:
1. Brush a baking pan with nonstick cooking spray oil; set it aside.

2. Mix the dry ingredients in a bowl; now, thoroughly combine the wet ingredients. Add the wet mixture to the dry mixture and mix until everything is well incorporated.

3. Select the "Bake" function and adjust the temperature to 330 degrees F. Press the "Start" key. When the display indicates "Add Food", place the baking pan on the air fryer tray.

4. Bake your blondies for 15 minutes or until a tester comes out clean when inserted in the middle.

5. Bon appétit!

Nutrition:
- Info288 Calories,20.2g Fat,22.6g Carbs,4.8g Protei.

Classic Chocolate Brownie

Servings: 6
Cooking Time: 20 Minutes
Ingredients:
- 1/2 cup almond meal
- 1/2 cup all-purpose flour
- 1/2 teaspoon baking powder
- 1/4 cup cocoa powder
- 1 cup brown sugar
- 1/2 cup butter, melted
- 2 large eggs
- 1 teaspoon vanilla extract
- A pinch of kosher salt

Directions:
1. Brush a baking pan with a nonstick cooking spray oil; set it aside.

2. Mix the dry ingredients, then, thoroughly combine the wet ingredients. Add the wet mixture to the dry mixture and mix until everything is well incorporated.

3. Select the "Bake" function and adjust the temperature to 330 degrees F. Press the "Start" key. When the display indicates "Add Food", place the baking pan on the air fryer tray.

4. Bake your brownie for 15 minutes or until a tester comes out clean when inserted in the middle.

5. Bon appétit!

Nutrition:
- Info318 Calories,21.5g Fat,28.5g Carbs,5.6g Protei.

Father's Day Croissants

Servings: 4

Cooking Time: 20 Minutes

Ingredients:

- 1 can refrigerated crescent rolls
- 1/2 cup chocolate spread
- 1/4 cup raisins, soaked in dark rum
- 1/4 cup almonds, chopped
- 1 large egg, whisked

Directions:

1. Separate the crescent rolls into eight triangles. Spread each triangle with chocolate spread, raisins, and almonds. Roll them up and lower them into the baking pan.
2. Brush the whisked egg on top of each croissant.
3. Select the "Air Fry" function and adjust the temperature to 350 degrees F. Press the "Start" key.
4. Air fry your croissants at 340 degrees F for about 15 minutes or until golden brown.
5. Bon appétit!

Nutrition:

- Info437 Calories,34.3g Fat,22.5g Carbs,10.4g Protei.

Easy Vanilla Donuts

Servings: 8

Cooking Time: 20 Minutes

Ingredients:

- 1 package refrigerated buttermilk biscuits
- 2 tablespoons butter, melted
- Vanilla glaze:
- 1 cup powdered sugar
- 2 ounces coconut milk
- 1 teaspoon pure vanilla extract

Directions:

1. Separate the biscuits and cut holes out of the center of each biscuit using a 1-inch round biscuit cutter; place them on parchment paper. Brush them with melted butter.
2. Select the "Air Fry" function and adjust the temperature to 350 degrees F. Press the "Start" key.
3. Lower your biscuits into the baking pan.

4. Air fry your biscuits at 340 degrees F for about 15 minutes or until golden brown, flipping them halfway through the cooking time.
5. Meanwhile, in a medium bowl, whisk together the powdered sugar, milk, and vanilla until smooth and creamy.
6. Dip the warm donuts into the vanilla glaze and enjoy!

Nutrition:

- Info222 Calories,8.4g Fat,31.7g Carbs,2.4g Protei.

Favorite Chocolate Lava Cake

Servings: 4

Cooking Time: 15 Minutes

Ingredients:

- 2 large eggs
- 1/2 stick butter, softened
- 4 ounces dark chocolate chunks
- 1/2 cup brown sugar
- A pinch of kosher salt
- A pinch of grated nutmeg
- 1/2 teaspoon ground cinnamon
- 2 tablespoons cocoa powder
- 4 tablespoons almond flour

Directions:

1. Select the "Air Fry" function and adjust the temperature to 375 degrees F. Press the "Start" key.
2. Brush four ramekins with nonstick spray.
3. Whisk the eggs with sugar until frothy. Add in the remaining ingredients and mix to combine.
4. Spoon the batter into the prepared ramekins and bake your lava cake for 10 minutes. Serve warm.

Nutrition:

- Info446 Calories,31.3g Fat,34.9g Carbs,8.1g Protei.

Authentic Cuban Tostada

Servings: 2
Cooking Time: 15 Minutes
Ingredients:

- 2 teaspoons butter
- 2 large eggs
- 2 tablespoons coconut milk
- 1/2 teaspoon vanilla extract
- 1/2 teaspoon ground cinnamon
- 1/3 cup brown sugar
- 4 slices thick white bread

Directions:

1. Select the "air fryer" function and adjust the temperature to 390 degrees F. Press the "Start" key.
2. In a mixing dish, whisk the butter, eggs, coconut milk, vanilla, cinnamon, and sugar.
3. Dip all the slices of bread in this mixture.
4. When the display indicates "Add Food", place the French toast in the air fryer oven pan.
5. Bake in the preheated air fryer for 10 minutes, turning them over halfway through the cooking time to ensure even cooking.
6. Enjoy!

Nutrition:

- Info338 Calories,10.9g Fat,46.4g Carbs,13.1g Protei.

Classic Cinnamon Tostada

Servings: 2
Cooking Time: 10 Minutes
Ingredients:

- 2 whole-wheat tortillas, cut into triangles
- 2 tablespoons brown sugar
- 1 teaspoon ground cinnamon
- 2 tablespoons butter, softened

Directions:

1. Select the "air fryer" function and adjust the temperature to 390 degrees F. Press the "Start" key.
2. Toss the tortilla chunks with the remaining ingredients.
3. When the display indicates "Add Food", place the French toast in the air fryer oven pan.

4. Bake in the preheated air fryer for 8 minutes, turning them over halfway through the cooking time to ensure even cooking.
5. Enjoy!

Nutrition:

- Info296 Calories,14.3g Fat,38.5g Carbs,4g Protei.

Cinnamon Waffle Sticks

Servings: 4
Cooking Time: 15 Minutes
Ingredients:

- 4 frozen waffles, cut into thirds
- 4 teaspoons butter, softened
- 1 tablespoon cinnamon powder
- 2 tablespoons agave syrup

Directions:

1. Select the "Air Fry" function and adjust the temperature to 350 degrees F. Press the "Start" key.
2. Air fry the waffles for about 3 minutes. Flip the waffles and continue to cook for 3 minutes.
3. Toss the waffle sticks with the butter, cinnamon, and agave syrup and serve immediately. Enjoy!

Nutrition:

- Info188 Calories,7.9g Fat,17.4g Carbs,2.3g Protei.

Old-fashioned Beignets

Servings: 6
Cooking Time: 20 Minutes
Ingredients:
- 1 can can refrigerated buttermilk biscuits
- 2 tablespoons butter, melted
- 1/2 cup chocolate hazelnut spread

Directions:
1. Separate the biscuits and place them on parchment paper. Brush them with melted butter.
2. Select the "Air Fry" function and adjust the temperature to 350 degrees F. Press the "Start" key.
3. Lower your biscuits into the baking pan.
4. Air fry your biscuits at 340 degrees F for about 15 minutes or until golden brown, flipping them halfway through the cooking time.
5. Dip the warm donuts into the chocolate spread and enjoy!

Nutrition:
- Info386 Calories,16.3g Fat,53.1g Carbs,6.9g Protei.

Grandma's Baked Apples

Servings: 6
Cooking Time: 20 Minutes
Ingredients:
- 6 medium apples, cored and sliced
- 2 tablespoons fresh lemon juice
- 2 teaspoons coconut oil, melted
- 1/2 cup brown sugar
- 1/2 teaspoon ground cardamom
- 1/4 teaspoon grated nutmeg
- 1 teaspoon ground cinnamon
- 1/2 teaspoon ginger, peeled and minced
- 2 tablespoons cornstarch

Directions:
1. Grease a baking pan with nonstick oil and set it aside.
2. Toss all the ingredients in the prepared baking pan.
3. Select the "Air Fry" function and adjust the temperature to 350 degrees F. Press the "Start" key. When the display indicates "Add Food", place the baking pan on the air fryer tray.
4. Bake the apples for about 15 minutes. Pierce the apples with a fork to ensure they are tender.
5. Enjoy!

Nutrition:
- Info187 Calories,1.8g Fat,45.1g Carbs,0.5g Protei.

Old-fashioned Walnut Brownies

Servings: 6
Cooking Time: 20 Minutes
Ingredients:
- 1/2 cup flour
- 2 tablespoons walnuts, chopped
- 1 teaspoon baking powder
- 1/2 cup butter, melted
- 1 cup brown sugar
- 1 teaspoon vanilla extract
- 2 eggs
- 1/2 cup cocoa powder

Directions:
1. Brush a baking pan with a nonstick cooking spray oil; set it aside.
2. Mix dry ingredients, then, thoroughly combine the wet ingredients. Add the wet mixture to the dry mixture and mix until everything is well incorporated.
3. Select the "Bake" function and adjust the temperature to 330 degrees F. Press the "Start" key. When the display indicates "Add Food", place the baking pan on the air fryer tray.
4. Bake your brownie for 15 minutes or until a tester comes out clean when inserted in the middle.
5. Bon appétit!

Nutrition:
- Info303 Calories,19.3g Fat,29.2g Carbs,5g Protei.

Key Lime Cheesecake

Servings: 9
Cooking Time: 25 Minutes
Ingredients:

- Crust:
- 8 ounces Oreos, crushed
- 6 tablespoons unsalted butter, softened
- 1/2 teaspoon ground cinnamon
- Filling:
- 20 ounces cream cheese
- 1 cup granulated sugar
- 1/2 cup double cream
- 4 large eggs
- A pinch of kosher salt
- A pinch of grated nutmeg
- 2 tablespoons freshly squeezed key lime juice
- 1/2 teaspoon coconut extract
- 1/2 teaspoon vanilla extract

Directions:

1. Select the "Air Fry" function and adjust the temperature to 400 degrees F. Press the "Start" key.
2. Mix all the crust ingredients; press the crust into a baking pan. Bake the crust for 6 minutes and allow it to cool on wire racks.
3. Using an electric mixer, whip the cream cheese, sugar, and double cream until fluffy; add one egg at a time and continue to beat until creamy; mix in the salt, nutmeg, key lime juice, coconut extract, and vanilla extract.
4. Pour the topping mixture on top of the crust. Bake your cheesecake at 390 degrees F for 15 minutes.
5. Allow your cheesecake to chill in your refrigerator before serving. Enjoy!

Nutrition:

- Info447 Calories,32.2g Fat,29.2g Carbs,7.6g Protei.

Baked Apples With Walnuts And Raisins

Servings: 4
Cooking Time: 20 Minutes
Ingredients:

- 4 large apples
- 1/2 cup old-fashioned rolled oats
- 1/4 cup walnuts, chopped
- 2 tablespoons coconut oil
- 1/4 cup brown sugar
- 1/2 teaspoon ground cardamom
- 1/2 teaspoon ground cinnamon
- 1/4 teaspoon ground nutmeg
- 1/8 teaspoon kosher salt
- 2 tablespoons raisins

Directions:

1. Use a paring knife to remove the stem and seeds from the apples, making deep holes.
2. In a mixing bowl, thoroughly combine the remaining ingredients. Divide the filling between the apples.
3. Select the "Air Fry" function and adjust the temperature to 350 degrees F. Press the "Start" key.
4. Bake the apples for 12 minutes and serve at room temperature. Enjoy!

Nutrition:

- Info307 Calories,11.2g Fat,57.2g Carbs,3.6g Protei.

Walnut Banana Bread

Servings: 7

Cooking Time: 20 Minutes

Ingredients:

- 2 cups all-purpose flour
- 1/2 cups ground walnuts
- 1 teaspoon baking powder
- 1 teaspoon baking soda
- 1/4 teaspoon kosher salt
- 1 stick butter, melted
- 1 cup brown sugar
- 2 ounces agave nectar
- 2 large eggs, whisked
- 4 medium ripe bananas, mashed
- 1/2 cup buttermilk

Directions:

1. Brush a baking pan with a nonstick cooking spray oil; set it aside.
2. Mix the dry ingredients; thoroughly combine the wet ingredients. Add the wet mixture to the dry mixture and mix until everything is well incorporated.
3. Select the "Bake" function and adjust the temperature to 330 degrees F. Press the "Start" key. When the display indicates "Add Food", place the baking pan on the air fryer tray.
4. Bake the banana bread for 15 minutes or until a tester comes out clean when inserted in the middle.
5. Bon appétit!

Nutrition:

- Info432 Calories,18.8g Fat,59.5g Carbs,7.8g Protei.

RECIPES INDEX

A

Almond Energy Bars 70

Asian-style Beef Bowl 33

Authentic Chicken Fajitas 53

Authentic Cuban Tostada 73

Authentic Indian Kofta 68

Authentic Kansas City Strip 27

Autumn Pumpkin Pancakes 66

B

Baked Apples With Walnuts And Raisins 75

Baked Pita Bread 17

Bbq Chicken Legs 51

Beef Brisket With Brussels Sprouts 31

Biscuits With Smoked Sausage 13

Blue Cheese Chicken Drumettes 50

Blue Cheese-crusted Filet Mignon 31

Breaded Filet Mignon 28

Brussel Sprout Chips 26

Buffalo-style Pizza 43

Buttery Roasted Carrots 60

C

Cabbage Steaks With Tofu 66

Carrot Puree With Herbs 67

Cashew Oatmeal Muffins 63

Cheese Broccoli Dip 23

Cheese Prawn Wontons 23

Cheese-stuffed Mushrooms 56

Cheesy Broccoli Tots 21

Cheesy Butternut Squash 61

Cheesy Egg Cups 14

Cheesy Roasted Parsnips 57

Chicken Fajita Salad 52

Chicken Sausage With Peppers 54

Chinese-style Rice Balls 41

Cinnamon Waffle Sticks 73

Classic Banana Beignets 15

Classic Beef Patties 32

Classic Breakfast Frittata 19

Classic Chicken Drumsticks 51

Classic Chicken Tacos 51

Classic Chocolate Brownie 71

Classic Cinnamon Tostada 73

Classic Fried Sea Scallops 36

Classic Homemade Cheeseburgers 29

Classic Parsnip Fries 21

Classic Porterhouse Steaks 30

Classic Toasted Sandwich 65

Classic Tortilla Chips 45

Classic Turkey Burgers 49

Corn Bacon Waffles 44

Crab And Pea Patties 34

Creamed Chicken Salad 52

Creole Catfish Fillets 38

Crispy Breaded Mushrooms 68

Crispy Pork Tenderloin 30

E

Easy Breakfast Granola 46

Easy Catfish Sandwiches 34

Easy Cinnamon Donuts 46

Easy Pepperoni Pizza 45

Easy Vanilla Donuts 72

Entrecôte Steak With Cauliflower 30

F

Fall Pumpkin Pancakes 18

Father's Day Croissants 72

Father's Day Fish Tacos 39

Favorite Cauliflower Tots 24

Favorite Chocolate Lava Cake 72

Favorite Halibut Steaks 34

Favorite Pizza Sandwich 16

Favorite Seafood Fritters 40

Festive Pork Butt 33

Festive Round Roast 33

Fluffy Almond Brownie Squares 70

Fried Breaded Portobellas 57

Fried Broccoli Florets 64

Fried Tofu With Sweet Potatoes 64

G

Garlicky Broccoli Florets 25

Golden Dijon Potatoes 56

Grandma's Apple Fritters 16

Grandma's Baked Apples 74

Grandma's Chicken Roulade 48

Grandma's Roasted Squash 55

Greek-style Fish Sticks 35

Greek-style Pita Pizza 19

Greek-style Quinoa Croquettes 41

H

Halibut Taco Wraps 35

Herb And Garlic Potatoes 61

Herbed Chicken Drumsticks 50

Herbed Roasted Zucchini 59

Herbed Salmon Steaks 38

Homemade Pâte à Choux 69

Homemade Pita Chips 43

Honey Apple Chips 20

Hot Chicken Drumettes 50

Hot Sardine Cutlets 38

I

Italian Cheese Sticks 23

Italian-style Cremini Mushrooms 65

Italian-style Eggplant 64

Italian-style Mini Pies 45

Italian-style Mushroom Patties 55

Italian-style Oatmeal Cheeseburgers 41

Italian-style Pulled Pork 27

J

Jamaican-style Pork 28

Japanese-style Yaki Onigiri 42

Juicy Turkey Breasts 48

K

Key Lime Cheesecake 75

Kid-friendly Cheese Bites 25

Kid-friendly Chicken Croquettes 49

Kid-friendly Chicken Nuggets 47

Kid-friendly Corn Muffins 66

L

Lemon-herb Sweet Potatoes 60

Lemony Sea Bass Fillets 37

Loaded Hash Browns 14

Louisiana-style Stuffed Chicken 48

M

Mediterranean Chicken Salad 53

Mediterranean-style Calzone 46

Mediterranean-style Cornbread Muffins 18

Mediterranean-style Fingerling Potatoes 63

Mexican-style Bulgur Patties 47

Mini Smoked Salmon Frittatas 37

Mom's Cheesy Biscuits 14

Montreal Chicken Drumettes 22

Mushroom And Oatmeal Fritters 44

Mustard Cheese Sandwich 18

O

Old Bay Pollock Fillets 36

Old-fashioned Beignets 74

Old-fashioned Walnut Brownies 74

Orange Chuck Roast With Baby Potatoes 28

P

Paprika Roast Turkey 49

Paprika Shrimp Salad 39

Parmesan Fennel Patties 60

Parmesan Pork Blade Chops 32

Peach Crumble Cake 69

Peppery Bean Dip 22

Peppery Breakfast Quiche 15

Pork And Sausage Patties 29

Q

Quiche Pastry Cups 42

Quinoa And Chickpea Meatballs 67

R

Rainbow Beet Salad 58

Red Beetroot Chips 24

Restaurant-style Fish Fingers 35

Restaurant-style Onion Rings 22

Roasted Baby Potatoes 58

Roasted Boston Butt 27

Roasted Brussels Sprouts 58

Roasted Buttery Eggplant 57

Roasted Garlic Cabbage 67

Roasted Golden Beets 62

Roasted Pepper And Cheese Bowl 55

Roasted Pepper Salad 59

Roasted Sweet Potatoes 59

Rosemary Roasted Potatoes 63

S

Sausage Wonton Wraps 24

Savory Herb Walnuts 21

Scotch Eggs With Sausage 16

Smoked Tempeh Sandwich 62

Smoky Carrot Dip 20

Spelt Burgers With Herbs 42

Spicy Creamed Beet Salad 62

Spicy Green Beans With Mushrooms 56

Spicy Oatmeal Patties 43

Sriracha Pork Burgers 31

Street-style Fish Fritters 39

Sweet Corn Muffins 13

T

Texas-style Fried Pickles 26

Thai-style Shrimp 36

The Best Cheese Broccomole 20

Toasted Greek Pita 45

Toasted Tortillas With Avocado 65

Traditional Greek Keftedes 29

Traditional Greek Tiganites 17

Traditional Japanese Korokke 25

Traditional Moroccan Brochettes 54

Traditional Polish Naleśniki 17

Turkey And Mushroom Croquettes 52

U

Ultimate Tuna Melts 40

V

Vanilla And Honey-roasted Peaches 70

Vanilla Maple Apricots 69

Vanilla Pear Beignets 15

Vanilla Walnut Blondies 71

Vegetable And Sausage Frittata 13

Vegetable And Scallop Skewers 37

W

Walnut Banana Bread 76

Wild Rice Patties 43

Printed in Great Britain
by Amazon